A Survey of Church History

Don Shackelford, Th.D.

Amridge University
Montgomery, Alabama

Amridge University Press
Turner School of Theology
1200 Taylor Road
Montgomery AL 36117

Revised and Augmented Edition

Printed in the United States of America

Publisher's Cataloging-in-Publication Data

Shackelford, Don, 1934—
A Survey of Church History / Don Shackelford
Five divisions, five appendices, Bibliography
96pp.
1. Church History 2. Apostasy—Reformation—Denominations 3. Restoration
I. Title.
ISBN: 978-1-61647-001-2
270

I dedicate this revised edition of
A Survey of Church History
to my dear, departed friend
and brother in the Lord
Dr. Rex A. Turner, Jr.
who departed this life August 11, 2008.
He was a great leader of
Amridge University for over 20 years.

And I heard a voice from heaven, saying,
"Write, 'Blessed are the dead
who die in the Lord from now on!'"
"Yes," says the Spirit, "so that they may rest
from their labors,
for their deeds follow with them."
Revelation 14:13

Preface to the Second Edition

A Survey of Church History that I wrote in 1961 has been out of print for several years. The original publishing company no longer exists. Its owner kindly consigned the copyright to me.

I was gratified by the response to the original edition. Churches used thousands of copies for the adult Bible classes. I still receive inquiries concerning it.

I have decided to publish this revised edition. I was twenty-six years old when I first compiled the material. Now, I am over seventy years of age. During these years I have served as a missionary to Italy, preached for several congregations, served as an elder, taught at Harding University for thirty years and I am currently teaching in the Bible programs of Amridge University in Montgomery, Alabama. I have continued to read widely on subjects of interest concerning the church and its history.

It is my fervent desire to be a faithful servant of the Lord. I desire to "sanctify Christ as Lord in your [my] hearts, always being ready to make a defense to everyone who asks you [me] to give an account for the hope that is in you [me], yet with gentleness and reverence" (1 Pet. 3:15). And "speaking the truth in love, to grow up in all aspects into Him, who is the head, even Christ" (Eph. 4:15). I confess that I have not always achieved these goals. But, if I know my heart, that is my earnest desire.

I am disturbed by what I perceive as attacks on the worthy goal of restoring New Testament Christianity today. The concept of truth is under severe attack today. Many consider all things to be relative and that truth cannot be known. Consequently, many young people, and some not so young, are joining community churches where their "needs can be met." Emotion has replaced a quest for truth in the minds of many people. Jesus' prayer to His Father is most relevant at this point: "Sanctify them in the truth; your word is truth" (John 17:17).

You will note that I have many long quotations in this booklet. I have done this because most people do not have access to the sources quoted. I have also used quotations from historians who are in denominations, but who correctly report events as they occurred.

I believe the Bible is the inspired Word of God. I hold that the New Testament is the only authority for Christian doctrine and practice. With the apostle Paul, I would urge you to "examine everything carefully; hold fast to that which is good" (1 Thess. 5:21). As Christians, let us be the "good soil" of Jesus' parable: "And the seed in the good soil, these are the ones who have heard the word in an honest and good heart, and hold it fast, and bear fruit with perseverance" (Luke 8:15).

Don Shackelford, Th.D.
Professor Emeritus, Harding University, Searcy, Arkansas
Professor, Amridge University, Montgomery, Alabama
Editor, Amridge University Press, Montgomery Alabama
June 4, 2010

Preface to the First Edition

The Cedar Crest Church of Christ in Dallas, Texas, initiated a new and different program for their Sunday morning adult classes in September 1961. A teacher rotation program was adopted whereby five teachers were assigned a subject that they would teach in each of the five adult classes.

My assignment was to teach a survey course in church history. The purpose of this study is to examine the history of the church from its establishment in the first century down to the present time. The study is suggestive, not exhaustive, in its scope.

As I began preparations to teach these lessons, I did not find a manual of church history adapted to our program. Most books covering the subject are entirely too tedious to be used in class situations. This manual is an attempt to provide a general outline of church history, using some materials that the average student might not have access to in his/her own library.

The footnotes will give credit to those sources from which material has been gleaned for this manual. I wish to thank the publishers who have given permission to quote from copyrighted sources. It is hoped that the student will want to investigate these sources for more complete information on the various points.

I do not claim to be a historian, and no doubt errors will be found in this booklet. I would be most appreciative to those who would call my attention to the same.

I express my appreciation to the elders of the Cedar Crest Church of Christ and Mrs. Grace Watson, our efficient church secretary, for encouragement and help in preparing the manuscript.

Don Shackelford
Dallas, Texas
December 22, 1961

Before We Begin

The material in this study naturally divides into four parts: (1) The New Testament Church; (2) The Apostasy that Resulted in Catholicism; (3) The Reformation that Resulted in Protestant Denominationalism; and, (4) The Restoration Movement. In this second edition, a fifth part is added: (5) Rediscovering the Restoration Plea.

Teachers should read through the manual to be acquainted with all the material before beginning the course of instruction. Particular points of importance should be noted for emphasis. A teacher may need additional preparation for class discussions.

Six weeks should be given in a detailed investigation of Part I: The New Testament Church. This will serve as a basis for comparison in subsequent studies. I have included "points to ponder" as a guide to consideration of what I believe are the most important items in each division. The teacher may want to add to these from time to time. Questions are added over the entire section at the conclusion of each major division. The teacher should find it helpful to refer to the material in the appendices.

Part II: The Apostasy That Resulted in Catholicism should also be studied for six class periods. Most of the practices of the denominations can be traced to innovations accepted from Roman Catholicism and transferred into the creeds of the reformers when they left the Catholic Church. It should be emphasized that the church historians quoted are *not* members of the church of Christ. They are recognized historians of the various protestant denominations.

Part III: The Reformation That Resulted in Protestant Denominationalism; and Part IV: The Restoration Movement, each can be taught in five class periods. The teacher may want to vary the length of time allotted to a particular section.

Part V: Rediscovering the Restoration Plea can be taught in two class periods. It can serve as a summary reflecting back to Part I.

I have found the "History of the Lord's Church" in *The Visualized Bible Study Series* by Jule Miller to be an excellent introduction to the course. It can be shown again as a conclusion of the study to reinforce learning. When I wrote the first edition (1961) little was available from scholars in churches of Christ. However, Everett Ferguson has written an excellent book you may wish to consult.[1]

Scripture quotations are from the New American Standard Bible, Updated Edition unless otherwise noted.

---

1 Everett Ferguson, *The Church of Christ: A Biblical Ecclesiology for Today.* (Grand Rapids, MI: William B. Eerdmans Publishing Company, 1996).

As you begin this study, I commend you "to Him who is able to do far more abundantly beyond all that we ask or think, according to the power that works within us, to Him *be* the glory *in the church* and *in Christ Jesus* to all generations forever and ever. Amen" (Eph. 3:20–21).

Outline

Before We Begin

Part I: The New Testament Church
  A. Definitions
  B. Designations in the New Testament for the Church
  C. When and Where the New Testament Church Began
  D. Organization and Government of the Church
  E. Creed and Discipline of the Church
  F. Worship in the New Testament Church
  G. How One Becomes a Member of the Church
  H. Unity of the Church
     Now Let's Review

Part II: The Apostasy That Resulted in Roman and Greek Catholicism
  A. Changes in Church Organization and in Church Government
  B. Apostasy in the Divinely Prescribed Worship of the Church
  C. Apostasy in the Designation of the Church
  D. Apostasy in the Doctrine and Practices of the Church
     Now Let's Review

Part III: The Reformation That Resulted in Protestant Denominationalism
  A. Early Attempts at Reform
  B. Immediate Causes of the Protestant Reformation of the Sixteenth Century
  C. Fundamental Principles of the Protestant Reformation Movement
  D. A Brief Study of the Lives and Doctrines of the Reform Leaders
     Now Let's Review

Part IV: The Restoration Principles and New Testament Christianity
  A. Four Basic Principles of the Restoration Movement
  B. Leaders in the Restoration of New Testament Principles of Christianity and Their Particular Contributions
  C. Division in the Restoration Movement Churches
     Now Let's Review

Part V: Rediscovering the Restoration Plea
    A. Obstacles to Rediscovering the Restoration Plea
    B. Characteristics Needed in Rediscovering the Restoration Plea
       Now Let's Review

Appendices

       Appendix A: A Study of the Greek Word ἐκκλησία from Which We Derive "Church"

       Appendix B: Early Ecumenical (General) Councils

       Appendix C: Who Shall Save Me?

       Appendix D: Origins of Denominations

       Appendix E: Last Will and Testament of the Springfield Presbytery

       Bibliography

Part I

The New Testament Church

As we study the church—apostasy from it and return to it—historically traced, it is important that we first understand what the New Testament church was as it began. James M. Tolle rightly noted:

> The church of Christ, as originally designed by Jesus, is a complete organization, divinely constituted. Since the Savior is its head (Col. 1:18) and the chief corner stone of its foundation (Eph. 2:19–20), only the characteristics He has set forth for it in His supreme authority, the New Testament are approved of God . . . The church is subject to Christ (Eph. 5:24). No authority was given by God to any man, set of men, or ecclesiastical body to change any of its features.[1]

A. Definitions

The New Testament has an abundance of teaching concerning every facet of the church. The word "church" or "churches" occurs in the New American Standard Bible, Updated Edition (NASBu) 110 times. It is found in Matthew, Acts, Romans, 1 and 2 Corinthians, Galatians, Ephesians, Philippians, Colossians, 1 and 2 Thessalonians, 1 Timothy, Philemon, Hebrews, James, 3 John, and Revelation.[2]

Our word *church* is derived from the Greek word *kyriakos*: "belonging to the Lord or Master."[3] It represents in our version of the New Testament the Greek word ἐκκλησία *(ekklesia)*.[4] Vincent notes that it is derived from εκ, "out," and καλέω, "call or summon."[5] The literal meaning of the term *ekklesia* is "a gathering of citizens called out from their homes into some public place; an assembly."[6]

---

1 James M. Tolle, *The Church, Apostasy, Reformation, and Restoration,* (pamphlet): 3.

2 For a complete examination of the word church see Appendix A.

3 *Webster's New Universal Unabridged Dictionary.* 2nd Ed. (New York: Simon & Schuster: 1979), 324.

4 William F. Arndt and F. Wilbur Gingrich, *A Greek-English Lexicon of the New Testament and Other Christian Literature.* 2nd Ed. Revised and Augmented by F. Wilbur Gingrich and Frederick W. Danker from Walter Bauer's Fifth Edition. (Chicago, IL: University of Chicago Press, 1958), 240.

5 Marvin R. Vincent, *Word Studies in the New Testament.* (Grand Rapids, MI: Wm. B. Eerdmans Publishing Company, 1946), 93.

6 Joseph Henry Thayer, *Greek-English Lexicon of the New Testament.* (Grand Rapids, MI: Zondervan Publishing House, n.d.), 195–196.

NOTES

The word *ekklesia* is used in the New Testament to designate an assembly of any kind:[7] 1. Christian: Acts 12:5; 14:27; 1 Corinthians 11:18, etc.; 2. Pagan: Acts 19:32–41; 3. Jewish: Acts 7:38; Hebrews 2:12.

In referring to the *ekklesia* of Christ, the word denoted: 1. The actual assembly of Christians;[8] 2. The church as the totality of Christians living in one place;[9] and, 3. The church universal to which all immersed believers are added.[10]

Points to Ponder

1. The word *church* in the original language means (a) a meeting place of Christians; (b) an assembly of people.
2. The word *church* as found in the Scriptures (a. always; b. never; c. sometimes) refers to a secular gathering.
3. The word *church* (a. is; b. is not) used in a universal sense as a designation of all immersed believers in Christ in the world.
4. One (a. can; b. cannot) properly compare the church of the New Testament with a denomination today.

B. Designations in the New Testament for the Church. The church is not given a proper name by inspiration, but is designated variously as:

(1) The body of Christ (Eph. 1:22–23); (2) The church of God (Acts 20:28); (3) Churches of Christ (Rom. 16:16); (4) Churches of the saints (1 Cor. 14:33); (5) Church of the first born *(ones,* ds) (Heb. 12:23); (6) The bride of Christ (Rev. 21:9; see also Eph. 5:22–33); (7) The family of God (Eph. 3:15); (8) The flock of God (1 Pet. 5:2); (9) The fold of Christ (John 10:16); (10) The general assembly (Heb. 12:23); (11) God's field, God's building (1 Cor. 3:9); (12) The house of Christ (Heb. 3:6); (13) The household of God, church of the living God, the pillar and support of the truth (1 Tim. 3:15); (14) A spiritual house (1 Pet. 2:5); (15) The temple of God (1 Cor. 3:16–17).

All of these designations serve to describe what the church is, and the various relationships it sustains with God and Christ. None of them is an exclusive title given by God to designate the church.

---

7 For an excellent explanation of the word *ekklesia* see: Everett Ferguson, *The Church of Christ: A Biblical Ecclesiology for Today.* (Grand Rapids, MI: William B. Eerdmans Publishing Company, 1996), 129–133.
8 Acts 12:5; 1 Corinthians 11:18; 14:4–5, 19, 28, 34–35; 3 John 6.
9 Acts 5:11; 13:1; 15:4; 2 Corinthians 1:1; 1 Thessalonians 1:2; 2 Thessalonians 1:1.
10 Romans 16:16; Matthew 16:18; Ephesians 1:22; 5:22–32.

Points to Ponder

1. True or False? The only Scriptural name of the church is "church of Christ."
2. The phrase "churches of Christ" (a. signifies; b. does not signify) different denominations in a province.
3. The phrase "church of the firstborn" (Heb. 12:23) refers to (a. Christians; b. Christ).
4. "Church of God" (a. would be; b. would not be) a Scriptural name to designate the church.

C. When and Where the New Testament Church Began
It is important that we have the date of the church's establishment fixed in our minds as we begin our study. This will facilitate distinguishing the divine institution of God from the humanly created institutions of men founded years later.[11]

The church is referred to by Christ Himself as the "kingdom" (Matt. 16:18–19); therefore, it is perfectly scriptural to apply the prophecies concerning the establishment of the kingdom to the establishment of the church, since they are one and the same thing.

1. Prophecies concerning the beginning of the church:
   a. Isaiah 2:2–3—The kingdom or church was to be established in the "last days," which is the New Testament period (Heb. 1:1–2; Acts 2:16–17). It would be established "as the chief of the mountains"; a prophecy concerning the pre-eminence of God's spiritual kingdom over all others. "All nations will stream to it," a reference to the universal character of the church (Matt. 28:19; Mark 16:16). It would be established when "the law will go forth from Zion and the word of the LORD from Jerusalem." This occurred on the first Pentecost after the resurrection of Jesus from the dead.[12]
   b. Daniel 2:31–45—In the interpretation of Nebuchadnezzar's dream, Daniel prophesied that the kingdom of God would be established during the fourth subsequent world kingdom:[13]
      (1) Babylonian kingdom—Nebuchadnezzar was king when the prophecy was uttered in 600 BC. His kingdom fell in 534 BC. It represented the head of gold.
      (2) Medo-Persian kingdom—It was established by Cyrus, king of Persia, and Darius, king of Media. It fell in 330 BC. It was represented by the breasts and arms of silver.

---

11 Study the chart: "The Kingdom/Church Established" by Maurice Tisdel on the next page.
12 Acts 1:4–8; 2:1–5, 47.
13 See the excellent discussion: Rex A. Turner, Sr., *Biblical Theology: Fundamentals of the Faith*. Rev. Ed., (Montgomery, AL: AmridgeUniversity Press, 2010), 408–414.

The Kingdom Church Established

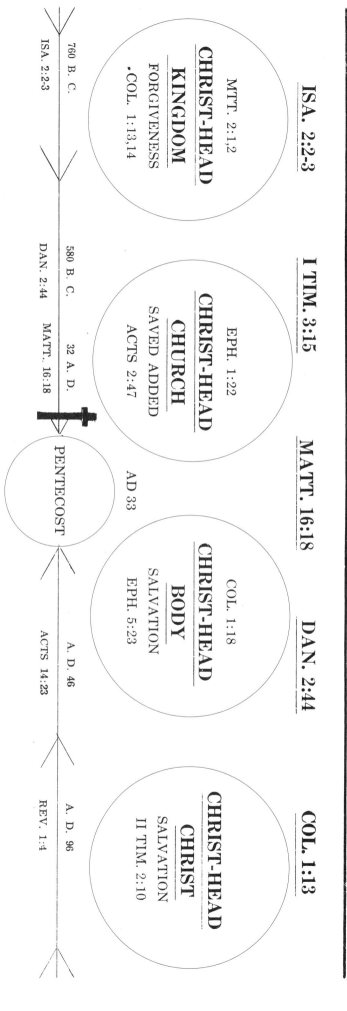

ISA. 2:2-3   I TIM. 3:15   MATT. 16:18   DAN. 2:44   COL. 1:13

MTT. 2:1,2
CHRIST-HEAD
KINGDOM
FORGIVENESS
·COL. 1:13,14

EPH. 1:22
CHRIST-HEAD
CHURCH
SAVED ADDED
ACTS 2:47

COL. 1:18
CHRIST-HEAD
BODY
SALVATION
EPH. 5:23

CHRIST-HEAD
CHRIST
SALVATION
II TIM. 2:10

PENTECOST

CHURCH
KINGDOM
BODY OF CHRIST
ALL SPIRITUAL BLESSINGS
FORGIVENESS OF SIN
SALVATION
EPH. 1:3

760 B. C.   580 B. C.   32 A. D.   AD 33   A. D. 46   A. D. 96

ISA. 2:2-3   DAN. 2:44   MATT. 16:18   ACTS 14:23   REV. 1:4

ACTS 1:5—2:47

WHEN?

A. D. 33

WHERE?

JERUSALEM

ISA. 2:2-3; ACTS 1:4-8; 2:47

(3) Greek kingdom—It was established by Alexander the Great, son of Philip of Macedon. At his death in 323 BC, the kingdom which he had carved out by his military genius was divided among his generals. It was represented by the belly and thighs of brass.

(4) Roman kingdom—It was established as a world power by Octavius Caesar in 30 BC. The Roman kingdom was represented by the legs and feet of iron and clay. "In the days of these kings" refers to the time of universal empires, and "it will crush and put an end to all these kingdoms, but it will itself endure forever" refers to the spiritual kingdom of the Lord established during the time of the Caesars of Rome.

c. Joel 2:28–32 Joel foretells the coming of the Messiah in a vivid way. The apostle Peter stood up on the day of Pentecost and said: "this is what was spoken of through the prophet Joel" (Acts 2:16).

These prophecies, as well as many others, were fulfilled when the first gospel sermon was preached by the apostles on the first Pentecost after the resurrection of Jesus.

2. During the Lord's ministry upon the earth, the church had not been established. Consider the following Scriptures: Mark 1:15; Matthew 6:9–10; 10:7; 16:28; 18:1–3; Luke 10:9; 22:16; and, Acts 1:6.

3. The church was established on the first Pentecost after the resurrection of Christ, at which time He began "adding to their number day by day those who were being saved" (Acts 2:47); He rescued "us from the domain of darkness, and transferred us to the kingdom of His beloved Son" (Col. 1:13). From that moment the church or kingdom was a reality.[14]

4. In conclusion, consider these syllogisms that settle the question of the precise time of the establishment of the church/kingdom:

Syllogism #1:
The kingdom was to begin when the law went forth from Jerusalem (Isaiah 2:2–3; Luke 24:47).
The law went forth from Jerusalem on the Pentecost after Jesus' resurrection (Acts 2:37–38).
Therefore, Pentecost was the beginning of the kingdom/church.

Syllogism #2:
The kingdom was to come with power (Mark 9:1).
The power came through the Holy Spirit on Pentecost (Acts 1:8; 2:1–40).
Therefore, the kingdom/church came on Pentecost.

---

14 See: 1 Timothy 3:15; Acts 5:11.

NOTES

Unless either the major or minor premise can be disproved, the conclusion of these syllogisms is inevitable. The church (or kingdom) began on the first Pentecost after Christ's crucifixion and resurrection.

Points to Ponder

1. It (a. is; b. is not) important to determine the date of the beginning of the church.
2. In Daniel's interpretation of Nebuchadnezzar's dream, the kingdom was to be established while (a. the Persians; b. the Romans; c. the Babylonians) were ruling.
3. The church (a. was; b. was not) established before Jesus' death.
4. The church (a. was; b. was not) established during the lifetime of John the Baptist.
5. It (a. is; b. is not) possible to determine whether the church and the kingdom are the same.
6. The church was established (a. on the first Passover; b. on the first Pentecost) after the resurrection of Christ.
7. The account of the church's establishment is recorded in (a. Acts 1; b. Acts 2).
8. The kingdom (a. will; b. will not) be established at the second coming of Christ.

D. The Organization and Government of the Church
The sole head and supreme ruler of the church is Jesus Christ.[15] No fallible man has ever been designated by God to be head of the church—all authority rests with Jesus Christ (Matt. 28:18).

During the infancy of the church, God set two special offices in the church: apostles and prophets (Eph. 4:11).[16] The prophets were God-appointed spokespersons. It was their special business to: 1. Predict future events (Acts 11:27–28; 21:10–11); 2. Reveal the counsels and purposes of God (Eph. 3:4–5); 3. Distinguish between the inspired Word of God and the uninspired teachings of men (1 Cor. 14:37; 1 John 2:20, 27); 4. Interpret the meaning of the Holy Scriptures, or the spoken oracles of God to edify the church (1 Cor. 14:1–4); 5. Disclose the secrets of the human heart (1 Cor. 14:23–25); and 6. Exhort, comfort, confirm, and edify (Acts 15:32; 1 Cor. 14:31).[17]

---

15 Colossian 1:18; Ephesians 1:20–23; 5:24.
16 See the chart: Organization of the Church Christ Built, on page 19.
17 To study this point further consult Robert Milligan, *The Scheme of Redemption.* (St Louis, MO: Christian Board of Publication, 1868). This old book has been reprinted and is a wonderful treatment of God's plan to redeem humankind after the fall of Adam and Eve. See also: Ferguson, 1996: 307–308.

ORGANIZATION OF THE CHURCH CHRIST BUILT

CHRIST
THE HEAD
Eph. 1:22

THE APOSTLE	THE HIGH PRIEST	THE SHEPHERD	THE OVERSEER
Heb. 3:1	Heb. 3:1	Heb. 13:20	1 Pet. 2:25

One Head
Hosea 1:11

One Body
1 Cor. 12:20

THE CHURCH — HIS BODY

ἐκκλησία   Eph. 1:22   Col. 1:18, 24   1 Cor. 12:27
Eph. 5:23   Col. 2:19

1. APOSTLES — FIRST SET
   ἀπόστολοι

2. PROPHETS — SECOND SET
   προφῆται

3. TEACHERS — THIRD SET
   διδάσκαλοι

   a. EVANGELISTS   Acts 21:8
      εὐαγγελίσται   2 Tim. 4:5

   b. PASTORS / ELDERS   BISHOPS (OVERSEERS)   STEWARDS   TO SHEPHERD
      ποιμένοι/πρεσβύτεροι   ἐπίσκοποι   οἰκόνομοι   ποιμάνειν

	BISHOPS (OVERSEERS)	STEWARDS	TO SHEPHERD
	Titus 1:5	Titus 1:7	Titus 1:7
	Acts 20:17	Acts 20:28	
	Acts 14:23	1 Tim. 3:2	

   DEACONS (MINISTERS, SERVANTS)
   διάκονοι (1 Tim. 3:8; Acts 6:1; Phil. 1:1)

4. PRIESTS   THE ELECT   LIVING STONES   THE FLOCK   GOD'S BUILDING
   ἱερεῖς

	THE ELECT	LIVING STONES	THE FLOCK	GOD'S BUILDING
	1 Pet. 1:1	1 Pet. 2:5, 9	Acts 20:28	1 Cor. 3:9
	Rev. 1:6	Rev. 5:10	Rev. 20:6	Eph. 2:21

Apostles were messengers especially selected by the Lord Himself (Matt. 10:1–4; Acts 1:16–26; Gal. 1:1, 15) to "make disciples of all the nations baptizing them in the name of the Father and the Son and the Holy Spirit, teaching them to observe all that I commanded you" (Matt. 28:18–19). They accomplished their mission by teaching and preaching the will of God. They also wrote God's will for us. It is called the New Testament. It is God's authority for the church through all ages. The apostles had no successors.

The New Testament gives no organization of the Lord's church other than that of the local, independent, autonomous congregation. No councils, synods, or conventions were ordained by Christ to govern His church. Lawrence Mosheim, a noted Anglican church historian wrote:

> The churches, in those early times, were entirely independent; none of them subject to any foreign jurisdiction, but each one governed by its own rulers and its own laws. For, though the churches founded by the apostles had this particular deference shown them, that they were consulted in difficult and doubtful cases; yet they had no judicial authority, no sort of supremacy over the others, nor the least right to enact laws for them. Nothing, on the contrary, is more evident than the perfect equality that reigned among the primitive churches; nor does there even appear in the first century, the smallest trace of that association of provincial churches, from which councils and metropolitans derived their origin. It was only in the second century that the custom of holding councils commenced in Greece, from whence it soon spread through the other provinces.[18]

The oversight of each local congregation was vested in a plurality of men called elders, pastors, or bishops—three different terms referring to the same persons. Elders (pastors or bishops) are to be appointed in each local church (Acts 14:23; Titus 1:5). It is their responsibility to:

1. Feed the flock spiritual food (Acts 20:28).
2. Guard the flock from false teachers (Acts 20:29–31).
3. Rule or exercise oversight of the church (1 Tim. 5:17; 1 Pet. 5:2).
4. Be examples, not lords over the church (1 Pet. 5:3).
5. Watch over souls as those who will give an account (Heb. 13:17).

Qualifications for elders (pastors, bishops) are given by the apostle Paul (1 Tim. 3:2–7; Titus 1:6–9). They have no authority over other congregations other than the one in which they are chosen to serve.

---

18 John Lawrence Mosheim, *Ecclesiastical History.* 2 vols. (Rosemead, CA: Old Paths Book Club, 1959), I, 30–31.

Deacons were also selected in congregations. From the association of the word with "overseers" (i.e., bishops) in Philippians 1:1, it may be concluded that deacons were special servants chosen for designated ministries. In fact the word *deacon,* derived from the Greek word διάκονος, *diakonos,* means "servant, attendant, minister."[19] In a general sense the deacon owes the same service to the Lord and bears the same responsibility as every other Christian. However, he has accepted a special responsibility of ministry. Qualifications are given for these special servants in 1 Timothy 3:8–13.

Two passages of Scripture may indicate that there were also special women servants in the church. In Romans, Paul said, "I commend to you our sister Phoebe, who is a servant of the church which is at Cenchrea; that you receive her in the Lord in a manner worthy of the saints, and that you help her in whatever matter she may have need of you; for she herself has also been a helper of many, and of myself as well" (16:1–2).[20] The word "servant" in verse one is *diakonon.* It cannot be ruled out that she was a special servant of the church,[21] however the preponderance of the use of this term in the New Testament is in a non-technical sense for those who serve.

The second passage having bearing on this subject is 1 Timothy 3:11: "Women must likewise be dignified, not malicious gossips, but temperate, faithful in all things." The Greek word γυναῖκας, *gunaikas,* can be translated "women or wives."[22] The question is: does this refer to special women servants or to the wives of deacons? Ferguson says, "No conclusive case can be made for deaconesses from these verses, nor can this position be ruled out. No biblical principle appears to prohibit the recognition of women in serving capacities in the church."[23]

Another group of Christian workers described in the New Testament are the evangelists. They are also called preachers or ministers.[24] As their name implies (Greek: εὐαγγελιστάς, *euangelistas*), they were men who proclaimed the gospel or good news[25] (Greek: εὐαγγέλιον, *euangelion*), the good news of redemption by the sacrifice of Jesus for humankind.[26]

---

19 G. Abbott-Smith, *A Manual Greek Lexicon of the New Testament,* 3rd Ed. (Edinburgh: T. & T. Clark, 1937), 108.

20 All Scripture quotations are from the New American Standard Bible, Updated Edition unless otherwise noted.

21 Ferguson, 1996: 338.

22 Ardnt and Gingrich: 168.

23 Ferguson, 1996: 339.

24 1 Timothy 2:7; Ephesians 6:21; 2 Timothy 4:5.

25 Romans 10:14–15.

26 Arndt and Gingrich: 317–318.

NOTES

It should be noted that the use of religious titles for ministers (including the apostles) such as "Father," "Reverend," "Holiness," "Cardinal," and "Pope" are without any foundation in the New Testament and are clearly foreign to its design.

Concluding this part of our study, it should be noted that to complete the review of the organization of the church, Christ's body, there must be brothers and sisters, all held in honor and esteemed by mutual affection, having the same care one for another. They are called: "a chosen race, a royal priesthood, a holy nation, a people for *God's* own possession" (1 Pet. 2:9). Other designations of Christians are: "chosen" (1 Pet. 1:1), "living stones" (1 Pet. 2:5), "the flock" (Acts 10:28), "fellow workers, God's field, God's building" (1 Cor. 3:9), and "members of the one body" (Eph. 3:6; 1 Cor. 12:12).

Points to Ponder

1. Scripture says the head of the church is (a. Christ; b. the Pope).
2. The two special workers in the church were (a. evangelists and teachers; b. elders and deacons; c. apostles and prophets).
3. It was the special work of the prophets (a. to work miracles; b. to reveal the counsels and purposes of God).
4. A church (a. should; b. should not) be autonomous.
5. Church historians (a. agree; b. disagree) on the point of local autonomy of the church.
6. The New Testament says the pastors were (a. preachers; b. bishops; c. elders).
7. Pastors/elders/bishops (a. must; b. should) be married according to the apostle Paul.
8. Pastors/elders/bishops (a. do; b. do not) have authority over congregations other than the one in which they are chosen to serve.
9. The word *deacon* denotes (a. an evangelist; b. a servant).

E. The Creed and Discipline of the Church
   The word *creed* is a derivation of the Latin word *credo* meaning "I believe." However, today, the word *creed* in popular usage is used synonymously as "discipline" or "rule" of practice of a religious body. For Christians there is only one discipline (rule of practice). It is the New Testament given by Christ for the purpose of guiding Christians in all the truth.[27]

---

27 2 Timothy 3:16-17; Galatians 1:11–12; John 20:30–31.

F. The Worship in the New Testament Church
What were the dominant characteristics of New Testament worship? Mosheim says, "The Christian religion was singularly commendable on account of its beautiful and divine simplicity."[28] A. H. Newman notes, "The worship of the early Christians was very free and informal."[29] These statements best describe the worship of God in the church of the first century. It was characterized by a beautiful and divine simplicity; being very free and informal. Another characteristic of the worship of the first century is that it consisted of *participation by all immersed believers* in:

1. Singing psalms, hymns and spiritual songs (Matt. 26:30; 1 Cor. 14:15; Eph. 5:19; Col. 3:16).
2. Praying (Acts 2:42; 12:5; 1 Thess. 5:17; 1 Cor. 14:15).
3. A memorial. Remembering the Lord's death, burial, and resurrection in the Lord's Supper (Matt. 26:26–29; Acts 20:7; 1 Cor. 10:16; 11:23–30).
4. A collection. They contributed into a common treasury of the church for the purpose of (1) providing for those in need (1 Cor. 16:1–2; 2 Cor. 8:1–5; 9:7–14), and (2) providing for those who preached the gospel (1 Cor. 9:7–14).
5. Preaching and teaching the Word of God (Acts 20:8, 18–21; 15:35; Col. 1:25).

The divinely approved day that the Lord designated for the Christians to assemble for worship is the first day of the week, Sunday (1 Cor. 16:2; Acts 20:7). It is also called "the Lord's day" (Rev. 1:10). That this day was *divinely appointed* is not questioned by those who accept *apostolic example* for their authority.
The Scripture not only prescribes the avenues of worship listed above but also the attitudes of acceptable worship:

1. It must be in spirit (John 4:24).
2. It must be done according to truth (John 4:24).
3. It must be done with thankfulness in the heart toward God (Col. 3:16).
4. It must spring from the depths of a sincere heart (Matt. 15:7–9).
5. It must be done with reverence and awe for God (Heb. 12:28).

---

28 Mosheim: I, 35
29 Albert Henry Newman, *Manual of Church History*. (Chicago: American Baptist Publication Society, 1957), 140.

NOTES

Points to Ponder

1. The worship of the first century church was characterized by (a. its formality; b. its simplicity).
2. New Testament worship included (a. singing; b. burning incense; c. saying the rosary; d. praying; e. observing the Lord's Supper; f. musical instruments).
3. True/False? The day Christians met to worship in the first century was the first day of the week.
4. Emphasis in worship of the New Testament is on (a. the pattern of truth; b. the attitude of the worshiper; c. both of the above).

G. How One Becomes a Member of the Church

No one ever *joins* the church established by Christ, but rather is *added* to it by the Lord upon his/her obedience to the Will of the Lord (Acts 2:41–47). The gospel of Christ must be accepted if one is to be saved. The gospel is received by believing (Mark 16:15–16); repenting of sins committed (Luke 13:3; Acts 2:38; Rom. 10:10; Acts 8:37); and, being immersed in water (Acts 8:38–39; Rom. 6:3–5; Col. 2:13; Gal. 3:27). Sinners who are smitten by God's love for them will not argue about the importance of any of the above factors over another in God's plan of salvation. They will gladly confess that *all of God's Will* is important for them.

Even those who deny that baptism (or immersion) is part of God's plan of salvation admit that it had that significance in the first century. Consider the following statement:

> It is most likely that in the Apostolic age when there was but "one Lord, one faith, and one baptism," and no differing denominations existed, the baptism of a convert *by that very act constituted him a member of the church,* and at once endowed him with all the rights and privileges of full membership (Emphasis mine, ds).[30]

This form (or pattern) of teaching was obeyed by everyone regardless of their nationality, social position or wealth (Rom. 6:17–18).

Points to Ponder

1. True/False? Man's obedience to God's commands does not nullify God's grace in salvation.
2. True/False? The New Testament never speaks of one *joining* the church of his choice.
3. Mark all correct answers: In order to be added to the church by the Lord one must: a. repent of sins; b. only believe,

---

30 Edward T. Hiscox, *The Standard Manual for Baptist Churches.* (Chicago: The American Baptist Publication Society, 1951), 22.

nothing more; c. be baptized; d. relate an experience of grace
to the congregation; e. confess Christ to be God's Son; f. pray
for God to save him; g. believe that Jesus is God's Son.

H. The Unity of the Church

Christ's church, according to its New Testament teaching, is
dedicated to the principle of unity of mind, doctrine, and practice.[31]
It abhors all division as sinful, a sign of carnality (1 Cor. 3:3–4),
and a work of the flesh (Gal. 5:19–20). Christians are commanded
to "keep an eye on those who cause dissensions and hindrances
contrary to the teaching which you [they] learned" from the apostle
Paul (Rom. 16:17–18). They are not to welcome or to aid "anyone
who goes too far and does not abide in the teaching of Christ"
(2 John 9–11). To seek peace and unity is an individual obligation
of every Christian as well as the church as a whole.[32]

Religious division with its many opposing systems and
divergent practices and doctrines is diametrically opposed to the
apostolic teaching in favor of unity and against division.

Points to Ponder

1. True/False? The New Testament church was united in
   doctrine, worship, and practice.
2. True/False? Division is a sign of carnality.
3. True/False? Persons should be received into Christian
   fellowship regardless of their beliefs.

Now Let's Review

Answer these statements as true or false without looking at the
material given in Part I. Then turn back and review the material and
see how many you answered correctly.

_____ 1. It is correct to refer to the church building as the church.

_____ 2. The word church may be used to designate any type of
assembly according to the Greek language.

_____ 3. The word church is used once in the New Testament to
refer to a mob.

_____ 4. The only scriptural name for the church is "church of
Christ."

_____ 5. The church was established during the ministry of John
the Baptist.

---

31 John 17:20–21; Romans 15:5–6; 1 Corinthians 1:10.
32 Ephesians 4:3; Philippians 2:3.

NOTES

_____ 6. The church and the kingdom are synonyms used to describe the same entity.

_____ 7. The "last days" refer to the period immediately before the second coming of Christ.

_____ 8. Daniel prophesied that the kingdom of Messiah would be established during the Roman period of world rule.

_____ 9. The only function of a prophet was to predict future events.

_____ 10. The only organization of the church (elders/deacons/Christians) is that of the local, autonomous congregation.

_____ 11. A plurality of pastors/overseers/elders was chosen to rule over each church in the first century.

_____ 12. The use of religious titles, such as "Father," "Reverend," "Holiness," is found in the New Testament.

_____ 13. The pastors/overseers/elders are told to "lord it over the flock of God."

_____ 14. The worship of the New Testament church was characterized by splendor and formality.

_____ 15. Attitudes of worship are as important as forms of worship.

_____ 16. The Lord's Supper is a memorial feast.

_____ 17. In the New Testament there is no example of one "joining" the church.

_____ 18. One may "join himself" to a local congregation.

_____ 19. Baptism is a part of God's demands in order that one may be saved.

_____ 20. God's New Testament law is uniform and must be obeyed by all people.

Part II

The Apostasy that Resulted in
Roman and Greek Catholicism

The seeds of apostasy were already being sown and the "mystery of lawlessness" was already at work during the first century of the church's existence.[1] The apostle Paul, in particular, warned of a general apostasy from the doctrine and practice given by Christ through the apostles to the church. Consider these warnings:

> Be on guard for yourselves and for all the flock, among which the Holy Spirit has made you overseers, to shepherd the church of God which He purchased with His own blood. I know that after my departure savage wolves will come in among you, not sparing the flock; and from among your own selves men will arise, speaking perverse things, to draw away the disciples after them. Therefore be on the alert, remembering that night and day for a period of three years I did not cease to admonish each one with tears. And now I commend you to God and to the word of His grace, which is able to build you up and to give you the inheritance among all those who are sanctified (Acts 20:28–32).

> Now we request you, brethren, with regard to the coming of our Lord Jesus Christ and our gathering together to Him, that you not be quickly shaken from your composure or be disturbed either by a spirit or a message or a letter as if from us, to the effect that the day of the Lord has come. Let no one in any way deceive you, for it will not come unless the apostasy comes first, and the man of lawlessness is revealed, the son of destruction, who opposes and exalts himself above every so-called god or object of worship, so that he takes his seat in the temple of God, displaying himself as being God. Do you not remember that while I was still with you, I was telling you these things? And you know what restrains him now, so that in his time he will be revealed. For the mystery of lawlessness is already at work; only he who now restrains will do so until he is taken out of the way. Then that lawless one will be revealed whom the Lord will slay with the breath of His mouth and bring to an end by the appearance of His coming; that is, the one whose coming is in accord with the activity of Satan, with all power and signs and false wonders, and with all the deception of wickedness for those who perish, because they did not receive the love of the truth so as to be saved. For this reason God will send upon them a deluding influence so that they will believe what is false, in order that they all may be judged who did not believe the truth, but took pleasure in wickedness (2 Thess. 2:1–12).

> But the Spirit explicitly says that in later times some will fall away from the faith, paying attention to deceitful spirits and doctrines of

---

1 2 Thessalonians 2:3, 7.

NOTES

demons, by means of the hypocrisy of liars seared in their own conscience as with a branding iron, men who forbid marriage and advocate abstaining from foods which God has created to be gratefully shared in by those who believe and know the truth. (1 Tim. 4:1–3)

I solemnly charge you in the presence of God and of Christ Jesus, who is to judge the living and the dead, and by His appearing and His kingdom: preach the word; be ready in season and out of season; reprove, rebuke, exhort, with great patience and instruction. For the time will come when they will not endure sound doctrine; but wanting to have their ears tickled, they will accumulate for themselves teachers in accordance to their own desires, and will turn away their ears from the truth and will turn aside to myths. (2 Tim. 4:1–4)

To these warnings by the apostle Paul, add the warning of Christ:

Then if anyone says to you, "Behold, here is the Christ," or "There He is," do not believe him. For false Christs and false prophets will arise and will show great signs and wonders, so as to mislead, if possible, even the elect. Behold, I have told you in advance (Matt. 24:23–25).

Also the warning of the apostle Peter:

But false prophets also arose among the people, just as there will also be false teachers among you, who will secretly introduce destructive heresies, even denying the Master who bought them, bringing swift destruction upon themselves. Many will follow their sensuality, and because of them the way of the truth will be maligned; and in their greed they will exploit you with false words; their judgment from long ago is not idle, and their destruction is not asleep (2 Pet. 2:1–3).

All of these Scriptures attest to the dark and ominous clouds of apostasy on the ecclesiastical horizon.

In the letters written to various congregations and individuals, scattered notices are given of the apostasy that was soon to take on larger proportions. Some were preaching a distorted gospel.[2] Judaizers were seeking to side-track Gentile Christians from the purity of the gospel by demanding they be circumcised and observe Moses' Law.[3] The spirit of division and sectarianism was causing division in at least one congregation.[4] Some were affirming that the resurrection was already past[5] or denying the reality of the resurrection altogether.[6] Some Christians were living immoral lives.[7]

Warnings were given to those who were forsaking the Christian assemblies[8] and to those who were eating the Lord's Supper in an

---

2 Galatians 1:6-9.
3 Acts 15:1; Galatians 5:1–4.
4 1 Corinthians 1:10-13; 3:3–9.
5 2 Timothy 2:18.
6 1 Corinthians 15:12–19.
7 1 Corinthians 5:1-3; 6:9–11.
8 Hebrews 10:25.

unworthy manner.[9] The apostle John warned churches that were spiritually indifferent and about to die.[10]

The apostasy involved many departures from the divine pattern of the New Testament. In Part II we will study several of them.

A. Changes in Church Organization and in Church Government

It was the apostle Paul who prophesied that from among the elders/pastors/overseers "men will arise, speaking perverse things, to draw away the disciples after them" (Acts 20:30). Developments in the second and subsequent centuries proved the veracity of this prediction because the first noticeable departure from the New Testament came in making a distinction between bishops (overseers) and presbyters (elders).[11]

One of the presbyters (elders) was chosen to preside over the meetings of the group, and soon began to be called the "president" or "presiding bishop":

> What we find existing in the second century enables us to infer, respecting the preceding times, that soon after the Apostolic Age the standing office of the president of the presbytery must have been formed; which president, as having preeminently the oversight over all, was designated by the special name of *Episkopos* (Bishop), and that distinguished from the other presbyters. Thus the name came at length to be applied exclusively to this presbyter, while the name presbyter continued at first to be common to all.[12]

Jacobs adds, "We begin to find congregations headed by a single officer for whom the name 'bishop' is exclusively reserved. The bishop becomes the most important man in the church. All the duties of administration are laid upon his shoulders."[13]

Newman illustrates how they sought to justify such a change from a plurality of bishops (overseers) in each congregation to a single bishop over a congregation:

> The distinction (between the bishop and presbyters) firmly established from the time of Cyprian, was brought about in the following way: The churches had come to be large bodies difficult to manage, especially in times of persecution. The collections and distributions of alms had assumed vast proportions, and the superintendence of this work

---

9 1 Corinthians 11:17–30.
10 Revelation 2:4; 3:2, 15–17.
11 "That they (presbyters) did not differ at all from the bishops or overseers, as is acknowledged by Jerome on Titus 1:5, . . . is evident from the fact that the two words are used indiscriminately, Acts 20:17, 28; Titus 1:5, 7, and that the duty of presbyters is described by the episkopein, 1 Peter 5:1–4." Thayer: 536.
12 Augustus Neander, *General History of the Christian Religion and Church,* 8th ed. Tr. Joseph Torrey. (Boston: Crocker & Brewster, 1847), I:190.
13 Charles M. Jacobs, *The Story of the Church.* (Philadelphia: The Muhlenberg Press, 1925), 19–20.

NOTES

devolved upon the Bishop. The Bishop was chairman of the board of presbyters and the leader of the church in the administration of discipline. Presbyters often disagreed, and the feeling grew that there should be in each Christian community a *center of authority*, whereby schism might be prevented and unity preserved. Occasions would frequently arise for the interference of the bishop, and *when the need for episcopal authority came to be felt, the vindication was sure to follow.*[14] (Emphasis mine, ds.)

Cyprian, Bishop of Carthage (AD 248–258), was a great promoter of episcopal rights, and it was he that defined that "the bishop was the representative (*antistes*) of Christ in the community over which he ruled, and therefore he had the authority over the single congregation or church which the Lord possessed over the universal church. He was the Lord or viceroy over that portion of God's heritage."[15]

The extension of the authority of the bishop over more than one congregation came as a result of the missionary activity of the bishop or the presbyters (elders) serving under his authority.

> The bishops who lived in the cities, had, either by their own ministry or that of their presbyters, erected new churches in the neighboring towns and villages. These churches, continuing under the inspection and ministry of the bishops, by whose labours and counsels they had been engaged to embrace the gospel, *grew imperceptibly* into ecclesiastical provinces, which the Greeks afterwards called dioceses. (Emphasis mine, ds)[16]

In time the bishops of the leading cities became elevated above their fellow bishops and were given the title of Metropolitans. Those of the major cities of Christendom: Rome, Alexandria, and Antioch; to which were later added: Ephesus, Jerusalem and Constantinople, were given the title of Patriarchs.[17]

Until the sixth century, there was no idea of a "universal bishop" presiding over all the bishops of the world. Strangely enough, it was not a bishop of Rome who first assumed the title of "universal bishop" or Pope. Mosheim writes:

> In the year [AD] 588, John, bishop of Constantinople, surnamed the Faster, on account of his extraordinary abstinence and austerity, assembled by his own authority, a council at Constantinople, to inquire into an accusation brought against Peter, Patriarch of Antioch; and upon this occasion, assumed the title of ecumenical or universal bishop.[18]

---

14 A. G. Newman, I:266.
15 T. M. Lindsay, *The Church and the Ministry in the Early Centuries*. (London: Hodder and Stoughton, 1903), 305.
16 Mosheim: I, 30.
17 Mosheim: I, 72; see also Newman: I, 314.
18 Mosheim: I, 145.

At that time, Gregory later called "the Great" was Bishop or Patriarch of Rome. He was greatly distressed by the presumption of his rival at Constantinople. Philip Schaff says:

> . . . Gregory I was provoked and irritated beyond measure by the assumption of his Eastern rival, and strained every nerve to procure a revocation of that title. He characterized it as a foolish, proud, profane, wicked, pestiferous, blasphemous, and diabolical usurpation, and compared him who used it to Lucifer. . . . After the death of John the Faster in 596, Gregory instructed his ambassador at Constantinople to demand from the new Patriarch, Cyriacus, as a condition of inter-communion, the renunciation of the wicked title, and in a letter to Maurice he went so far as to declare, that "Whoever calls himself universal priest, or desires to be called so, was the forerunner of Antichrist."[19]

After the death of Gregory the Great, the Roman Patriarch, Boniface III, assumed the title his predecessor had so vehemently rejected. Mosheim writes:

> The disputes about pre-eminence, that had so long subsisted between the bishops of Rome and Constantinople, proceeded, in this century [the seventh, ds] to such violent lengths, as laid the foundations of that deplorable schism, which afterwards separated the Greek and Latin churches . . . Boniface III engaged [the emperor] Phocas, that abominable tyrant . . . to take from the bishop of Constantinople the title of ecumenical or universal bishop, and to confer it upon the Roman pontiff . . . thus was the papal supremacy first introduced.[20]

This presumption has continued unabated to the present day. In AD 1870 the First Vatican Council declared that the Roman Bishop is infallible in matters of doctrine and morals when speaking "ex cathedra."[21] The schism between the Greek Orthodox and Roman Catholic Church continues to this day due in large part to the matter of primacy.

Commensurate with this growth in the power of the bishop was a change of concept in the Christian ministry. At first all Christians were regarded as equals. Men who preached the gospel were called evangelists. However, they were not regarded as having special rights or privileges. But in the fourth century, definite distinctions were being drawn between the minister and other Christians. The word "clergy"[22] that was formerly used to designate the entire body of Christians came to be applied only to the

19 Philip Schaff, *History of the Christian Church.* 8 Vols. (Grand Rapids: W. B. Eerdmans Publishing Company, 1953), III, 220.
20 Mosheim: I, 160.
21 Ex Cathedra is Latin for "from the chair," i.e. the seat of authority in St. Peter's Cathedral in Rome.
22 "Clergy" is from the Greek word κλήρος, *kleros*, "that which is assigned by lot, portion, share." It is used in 1 Peter 5:3 "to denote the 'flock' as a whole, i.e., the various parts of the congregation." Ardnt and Gingrich: 435.

NOTES

ministers. The word "laity" (from the Greek word λαός, *laos,* "the people, mass, crowd")[23] came to be used for Christians not serving as ministers. The "clergy" came to have the exclusive task of preaching the word and administering "the sacraments."[24]

The historian Mosheim describes this development:

> Even the bishops themselves, whose opulence and authority were considerably increased since the reign of Constantine, began to introduce gradually, innovations into the forms of ecclesiastical discipline, and to change the ancient government of the church. Their first step was an entire exclusion of the people from all part in the administration of ecclesiastical affairs; and afterwards, they by degrees divested even the presbyters of their ancient privileges, and their primitive authority, that they might have no importunate protestors to control their ambition, or oppose their proceedings; and principally, that they might either engross to themselves, or distribute as they thought proper, the possessions and revenues of the church. Hence it came to pass that, at the conclusion of this century [fourth], there remained no more than a mere shadow of the ancient government of the church. Many of the privileges, which had formerly belonged to the presbyters and people were usurped by the bishops; and many of the rights, which had been formerly vested in the universal church, were transferred to the emperors, and to subordinate officers and magistrates.[25]

Another apostasy initiated during the first four centuries and which did much to displace the New Testament from its rightful place as the only rule of faith and practice in the church was the growth of councils. During the apostolic age, all questions were decided by a "thus says the Lord." The early writings of the Christian leaders show the reverence and respect they had for Scripture during the first two centuries. Cyprian, bishop of Carthage, was the principal promoter of a transference of authority from the Word of God to the councils of the church:

> His practical thought was that as each bishop sums up in himself the church over which he presides, the whole church of Christ practically exists in the whole of the bishops, and the harmonious action of the whole church can be expressed through the common action and agreement of the bishops.[26]

This gave authority to the meetings of bishops from the various cities of the province. The meetings were called church councils.

> The provincial bishops assembled in council, deliberated together concerning those matters that related to the interest of the churches of a whole province, as also concerning religious controversies, the forms, and rites of divine service, and other things of like moment.[27]

---

23 Ardnt and Gingrich: 466.
24 Schaff: II, 121 and Jacobs: 19.
25 Mosheim: I, 93.
26 Lindsay: 314.
27 Mosheim: I, 93.

It is to the Emperor Constantine that credit must be given for an extension of the power of councils beyond the provincial limit:

> Down to the time of Constantine, the general organization has gone no further than the provinces. It was Constantine who extended it. On rare occasions there had been meetings which were attended by the bishops of several provinces. In [AD] 325, Constantine determined to hold a synod of the Empire. The church had become his church, and with the statesman's love of organization, he desired it to be one church, with a single law-making body, with uniform practices and a single creed. The general (or ecumenical) council was to be the law-making body, and was to establish uniformity, in doctrine and in practice, throughout the Empire.[28]

The first general council was held at Nicea in AD 325 and was presided over by Constantine. Philip Schaff notes:

> The emperors after Constantine (as the popes after them) summoned the general councils, bore the necessary expenses, presided in the councils through commissions, gave to the decisions in doctrine and discipline the force of law for the whole Roman Empire, and maintained them by their authority. The emperors nominated or confirmed the most influential metropolitans and patriarchs.[29]

In conclusion, as Schaff says, "The apostolical organization of the first century now gives place to the old Catholic episcopal system; and this in turn, passes into the metropolitan, and after the fourth century into the patriarchal."[30] Therefore, by the end of the fourth century there remained no more than a mere shadow of the New Testament government of the church of the Lord.

Points to Ponder

1. The apostle (a. Peter; b. Paul; c. James) gave many warnings in his writings concerning the apostasy which was to come.
2. The apostasy (a. had; b. had not) begun in the first century.
3. The apostasy was to begin (a. among the evangelists; b. among the deacons; c. among the elders).
4. Distinctions between the "presbyters/elders" and "bishops/overseers" arose in this century: (a. first; b. second; c. third).
5. (a. Paul; b. Augustine; c. Cyprian) was a great promoter of episcopal rights.
6. In the course of time, the bishops of the largest and most influential cities of the empire were called (a. deacons; b. popes; c. patriarchs).

---

28 Jacobs: 36 (See also: Mosheim: I, 93.)
29 Schaff: II, 120; for the most important early general or ecumenical councils and their doctrinal decisions consult Appendix B.
30 Schaff: III, 135.

NOTES

7. The first man to assume the title of Pope (Universal Bishop) was (a. Boniface III of Rome; b. John, bishop of Constantinople; c. James, bishop of Jerusalem).
8. The bishop who vehemently denounced the use of such a title as "Universal Bishop" was (a. John of Constantinople; b. Gregory of Rome).
9. The first Roman bishop to assume the title of Pope (Universal Bishop) was (a. Gregory; b. Boniface).
10. The Roman Pope was declared infallible by (a. the apostles; b. a council in AD 240; c. a council in AD 1870).
11. The evangelists and ministers of the first century (a. were; b. were not) called "clergy."
12. The Roman Emperor responsible for the structural organization of the early Roman and Greek Catholic churches was (a. Nero; b. Vespasian; c. Constantine).
13. The assemblies of bishops/overseers from various cities of the empire were called (a. councils; b. lectureships).
14. Most of the changes in the government of the church were accomplished by the (a. second; b. third; c. fourth) century.

B. Apostasy in the Divinely Prescribed Worship of the Church
    The worship of the church of the first century which I have in another place described as having had a beautiful and divine simplicity was not destined to continue without alteration. Even in the second century AD, innovations began to be introduced. Lawrence Mosheim pointedly declares:

> There is no institution so pure and excellent which the corruption and folly of man will not in time alter for the worse, and load with additions foreign to its nature and original design. Such in a particular manner, was the fate of Christianity. In this century [the second], many unnecessary rites and ceremonies were added to the Christian worship, the introduction of which was extremely offensive to wise and good men. These changes, while they destroyed the beautiful simplicity of the gospel, were naturally pleasing to the gross multitude, who are more delighted with the pomp and splendour of external institutions, than with the native charms of rational and solid piety, and who generally give little attention to any objects but those which strike their outward senses.[31]

He further explains some causes that led to apostasies in worship:

*   Bishops augmented the number of religious rites in the Christian church, by way of accommodation to the infirmities and prejudices both of Jews and heathens, in order to facilitate their conversion to Christianity. This addition of external rites was also designed to remove the

---

31 Mosheim: I, 55.

opprobrious calumnies which the Jewish and pagan priests cast upon the Christians, on account of the simplicity of their worship, esteeming them little better than Atheists, because they had no temples, altars, victims, priests, nor anything of that external pomp in which the vulgar are so prone to place the essence of worship.

• The profound respect that was paid to the Greek and Roman mysteries, and the extraordinary sanctity that was attributed to them, was a further circumstance that induced the Christians to give their religion, in order to put it upon an equal foot, in point of dignity, with that of the Pagans. The custom of teaching their religious doctrines by images, actions, signs, and other sensible representations which prevailed among the Egyptians was another cause of the increase of external rites in the church.[32]

Thus, as one can easily recognize, the changes may be attributed to a "paganizing influence upon Christianity." This corruption of Christian worship was gradual until AD 325, at which time, the flood gates of apostasy were opened wide to religious invention by the supposed conversion of Emperor Constantine. When the pagan emperor became a "Christian" emperor, the pagan empire, by virtue of the change in its ruler, became a "Christian" empire. Church historians are almost unanimous in their opinion of the harmful effects of this union of church and state. Philip Schaff sums up the consensus of opinion:

> These evil results may be summed up under the general designation of the secularization of the church. By taking the whole population of the Roman Empire the church became, indeed, a church of the masses, a church of the people, but as the same time more or less a church of the world. Christianity became a matter of fashion . . . with the secularizing process, therefore, a paganizing tendency went hand in hand.[33]

Newman adds:

> When he [Constantine] offered temporal inducements to the profession of Christianity, he not only brought multitudes of unregenerate people into the churches, but he also aided in making it a part of public opinion to regard the profession of Christianity as a mere form, and to attach a magical significance to the ordinances. . . . Christianity was secularized. The doors of the church were thrown open so wide, that the distinction between Christianity and the world was obliterated.[34]

---

32 Mosheim: I, 56–57.
33 Schaff: III, 125–126.
34 Newman: 313.

NOTES

Some of the more striking apostasies in worship were:

1. The Lord's Supper. The apostles and early Christians observed the Lord's Supper each Sunday as a simple memorial feast. The changes came gradually. They included:

   a. The prayers, used upon this occasion, were lengthened; and the solemnity and pomp, with which this important institution was celebrated, were increased . . . gold and silver vessels were now [third century] used in the administration of the Lord's Supper.[35]

   b. In the fourth century, the Lord's Supper came to be observed in some places two or three times a week. It was also commemorated at the tombs of martyrs and at funerals, "which custom gave rise to the masses that were afterwards performed in honor of the saints and for the benefit of the dead."[36]

   c. In the thirteenth century, the mass (no longer being called the Lord's Supper) was declared to be a "literal sacrifice" of the body and the blood of Christ. It was at the Catholic Council of Trent that the doctrine of the literal sacrifice (called transubstantiation) became a dogma of faith. I have in my files a Catholic wall poster, copies of which I saw frequently in Italy, that reads: "Christ is offered every day for our sins." Williston Walker wrote:

      > About [AD] 831, Paschasius Radbertus, a monk of the monastery of Corbie, near Amiens, of remarkable learning in Greek as well as in Latin theology, set forth the first thorough going treatise on the Lord's Supper, "De Corpore et Sanguine Domini." In it he taught, with Augustine, that only those who partake in faith eat and drink the body and blood of Christ . . . And also that by divine miracle the substance of the elements is made the very body and blood of Christ.[37]

   d. Tertullian reasoned that in order to offer a sacrifice there must be a priest. He introduced the term *sacerdos* (priest) into full use.[38]

   e. In the year AD 1415, the cup of the Lord's Supper was denied to the "laity" (i.e., the masses). However, in recent years the Roman Catholic Church has restored the practice of allowing the laity to drink the cup.

---

35 Mosheim: I, 79.
36 Mosheim: I, 152.
37 Williston Walker, *A History of the Christian Church.* Revised by Cyril Richardson, Wilhelm Pauck and Robert Handy. (New York: Charles Scribner's Sons, 1959), 192.
38 Walker: 91.

Thus, in the course of just a few hundred years, the Lord's Supper was corrupted from the simple memorial feast into a pompous observance of the "real sacrifice" of Christ, presided over by a priest dressed in splendid robes. Should the apostles of Christ see the mass today, they would not recognize at all what was occurring.

2. Music. The divinely ordained worship in song was corrupted by the addition of musical instruments. These were introduced by Roman churches in the seventh century AD. Philip Schaff says, "The use of organs in churches is ascribed to Pope Vitalian (657–672)."[39]

Protestant scholars of the nineteenth century were very frank in their admission that instruments of music in Christian worship had no biblical foundation at all. Those who seek to introduce them into worship today would do well to ponder the fact that their only "authority" for doing so goes back to the Roman Catholic Church! Listen to the powerful words of one of the Methodist's greatest Bible commentators:

> I further believe that the use of such instruments of music, in the Christian Church, is *without* the *sanction* and *against* the *will* of God; that they are subversive of the spirit of true devotion, and that they are *sinful....* I am an old man, and an old minister, and I here declare that I never knew them productive of any good in the worship of God; and have reason to believe that they were productive of much evil. Music, *as a science*, I esteem and admire; but instruments of music *in the house of God* I abominate and abhor. This is the abuse of music; and here I register my protest against all such corruptions in the worship of the Author of Christianity. The late venerable and most eminent divine, the Rev. *John Wesley*, was a *lover of music*, and an *elegant poet*, when asked his opinion of instruments of music being introduced into the chapels of the Methodists said, in his terse and powerful manner, "I have no objections to instruments of music in our chapels, provided they are neither HEARD nor SEEN." I say the same, though I think the expense of purchase had better be spared.[40]

3. Veneration (worship) of saints.[41] The veneration of Mary, the mother of Jesus, and of other "saints" that the Catholic Church

---

39 Schaff: IV, 439. For those wishing to pursue further study of instrumental music in the worship, I suggest that you read: M. C. Kurfees, *Instrumental Music in the Worship.* (Nashville: The Gospel Advocate Company, 1950).

40 Adam Clarke, *Commentary and Critical Notes on the Bible.* 6 Vols. (Nashville: Abingdon Press, n.d.), IV: 684.

41 It should be noted that the use of the word "saint" in this part of our study is according to the current Roman Catholic usage and not according to the primary biblical meaning of the word. According to their dogma, a saint is defined as one whose life was characterized by extreme piety, asceticism or who had given himself/herself as a martyr for Christ. But to be worshipped, this person must meet certain qualifications: (1) Be dead; (2) Have performed

NOTES

has created is another direct influence of paganism upon the history of Christianity. This veneration that the Catholic Church has evolved can be traced, in its inception, to the anniversary celebrations of the death of Christian martyrs: "The beginnings of the veneration of martyrs and of their relics run back to the middle of the second century. Their deaths were regularly commemorated with public service."[42]

The "conversion" of Constantine and the resulting inclusion of masses of pagans into the church gave impetus to this practice.

> With the conversion of Constantine . . . and the accession to the church of masses fresh from heathenism, this reverence largely increased. Constantine himself built a great church in honor of Peter in Rome. His mother, Helena, made a pilgrimage to Jerusalem, where the true cross was thought to be discovered. . . . Popular opinion, which has long sanctioned the remembrance of martyrs in prayer and worship, had passed over, before the close of the fourth century, to the feeling that they were to be prayed to as intercessors with God, and as able to protect, heal, and aid those who honored them. . . . The martyrs, for the masses, took the place of the old gods and heroes. To the martyrs, popular feeling added distinguished ascetics, church leaders, and opponents of heresy. . . . They were guardians of cities, patrons of trades, curers of disease. They are omnipresent . . . they were honored with burning tapers.[43]

An example of this process of paganization can be seen in its evolvement in the case of Mary, the Lord's mother. Curiously enough, she did not stand out preeminent until well into the fourth century. Schaff remarks:

> The "mother of the Lord" was transformed into a "mother of God," humble "handmaid of the Lord" into a "queen of heaven," the "highly favored" into a "dispenser of favors," the "blessed among women" into the "intercessor above all women," nay, we may almost say, the redeemed daughter of fallen Adam, who is nowhere in Holy Scriptures excepted from the universal sinfulness, into a sinlessly holy co-redeemer.[44]

In AD 1854, the Roman Pope issued a command that Catholics must believe in the immaculate conception of Mary.

---

at least two miracles while living; (3) Have performed at least two other miracles by his/her intercession after death. Today the Pope is the only one who can "beatify" and "canonize" a saint. They attempt to dodge the charge of idolatry by ascribing to "saints" a lesser worship than that ascribed to God, but in actual practice, which I have frequently observed in Italy, one would judge the opposite to be true. Consult *The Catholic Encyclopedia,* s.v. "Beatification and Canonization," II:364-369.

42 Walker: 155.
43 Walker: 155.
44 Schaff: III, 441.

In AD 1950, Pope Pius XII declared that Mary was "assumed" into heaven: body, soul, and spirit.

4. The veneration of the relics of saints. Closely connected with the veneration of saints is the veneration attached to things that had been associated with them.

> The veneration of martyrs and saints had respect, in the first instance to their immortal spirits in heaven, but came to be extended, also, in a lower degree, to their earthly remains or relics. By these are understood, first, their bodies, or rather parts of them, bones, blood, ashes; then all which was in any way closely associated with their persons, clothes, staff, furniture, and especially the instruments of their martyrdom. After the time of Ambrose [AD 339–397] the cross of Christ also, which with the superscription and nails, are said to have been miraculously discovered by the empress Helena . . . was included and subsequently His crown of thorns, and His coat, which are preserved . . . according to legend . . . in Paris and in Treves.[45]

The wide-spread use of relics is illustrated by one of the statutes of the Seventh General Council that was convened in AD 787. It reads as follows: "If any bishop from this time forward is found consecrating a temple without holy relics, he shall be deposed as a transgressor of the ecclesiastical traditions."[46]

5. Festivals. In addition to the festivals instituted in memory of each of the saints, others were introduced to commemorate special doctrines or events in the Catholic calendar.
   a. Festivals of the lance, nails and crown of thorns: Innocent V instituted festivals sacred to the memory of the *lance* with which our Saviour's side was pierced, the *nails* that fastened him to the cross, and the *crown of thorns* he wore at his death."[47]
   b. Purification of the Blessed Virgin
      In the sixth century the festival of the purification of the Blessed Virgin, was invented with a design to remove the uneasiness of the heathen convert on account of the loss of their Lupercalia, or feast of Pan, which was formerly observed in the month of February, the festival of the immaculate conception, the day set apart to commemorate the birth of St. John, and others less worthy of mention.[48]
   c. The festival of Christmas. One of the grandest of pagan festivals was converted into one of the greatest "Christian" festivals: the observance of the 25th of December.

> December 25 was a great pagan festival, that of *Sol Invictus*, which celebrated the victory of light over darkness and the

45 Schaff: III, 449–450.
46 *Catholic Encyclopedia*, s.v. "Second Council of Nicea," II: 841.
47 Mosheim: I, 371.
48 Mosheim: I, 153.

lengthening of the sun's rays at the winter solstice. The assimilation of Christ to the sun god, as Sun of Righteousness, was widespread in the fourth century and was furthered by Constantine's legislation . . . which *is not unrelated to the fact that the sun god was the titular divinity of his family.* [Emphasis mine, ds] The gift-giving we associate with Christmas has its origin partly in the similar custom at the Roman Saturnalia.[49]

6. Other innovations.
   a. The sign of the cross.

   > This arose, as early as the second century, the custom of making the sign of the cross on rising, bathing, going out, eating, in short, one engaging in any affairs of every-day life; a custom probably attended in many cases even in that age, with the superstitious confidence in the magical virtue of this sign. . . . The crucifix, that is the sculptured or carved representation of our Saviour attached to the cross, is of much later date, and cannot be clearly traced beyond the middle of the sixth century.[50]

   b. The use of Holy Water: "Protection against the power of the devils was sought in the use of sacred objects . . . a few drops of holy water . . . was believed to afford protection."[51]
   c. The counting of prayers with rosary beads:

   > There are also to be found in this age [Tenth Century], manifest indications of the institution of the rosary and crown of the Virgin, by which her worshippers were to reckon the number of prayers that they were to offer this new divinity. . . . the rosary consists of fifteen repetitions of the Lord's prayer, and six or seven times, salutations of Ave Marias.[52]

Points to Ponder

1. Mosheim lists (a. two; b. four; c. ten) causes for changes in worship.
2. The main reason for changes in worship may be attributed to (a. bringing the worship up to date; b. eliminating Jewish influences; c. paganizing influences upon Christianity).
3. The Roman Emperor (a. Augustus; b. Nero; c. Constantine) was largely responsible for the beginning of these innovations in worship.
4. The Roman Catholic doctrine that the unleavened bread and the fruit of the vine are changed into the literal body and blood of Christ is called (a. Mass; b. Consubstantiation; c. Transubstantiation).

---

49 Walker: 155.
50 Schaff: II, 269.
51 Jacobs: 179.
52 Mosheim: I, 229.

5. The observance of the Lord's Supper on other days than Sunday began in the (a. first; b. fourth; c. tenth) century.
6. The denial of the cup to the laity was made official in AD (a. 831; b. 1415; c. 1948).
7. The introduction of musical instruments into Christian worship is attributed to (a. Christ; b. the apostles; c. Pope Vitalian).
8. Some protestant scholars of the last century (a. sanctioned; b. rejected) instruments of music in worship.
9. The biblical and Roman Catholic definition of "saints" (a. is; b. is not) the same.
10. The saints are considered by Catholics to be (a. inferior beings; b. intercessors with God; c. taking the place of Christ).
11. True/False? A relic may be anything closely connected with the person of a saint.
12. The observance of Christmas had its origin in (a. New Testament times; b. later centuries).
13. Pagans associated an observance of December 25th with the god of (a. rain; b. harvest; c. sun).
14. Making the sign of the cross goes back to (a. the tenth; b. the eighth; c. the second) century.
15. The use of Holy Water began in the (a. apostolic church; b. later belief that it protected against devils).
16. The use of rosary beads in prayer may be traced to the (a. fifth; b. tenth; c. fifteenth) century.

C. Apostasy in the Designation of the Church
We have already studied designations in Scripture used to describe the church. The appellation "Catholic" was added in the latter part of the second century as a descriptive term of the universality of the church. Ignatius [AD 110–117] was the first to employ it extensively. Williston Walker describes it as a "technically descriptive adjective, almost the equivalent of 'orthodox,' [that] gradually became common."[53]

To the name "Catholic," later generations added "Roman" or "Greek," and "Holy" and "Apostolic." That the church bearing that title today is "Catholic" (i.e., universal); and "Roman" (in origin), none would deny. But that it is "holy" and "apostolic" are not true.

D. Apostasy in the Doctrine and Practices of the Church
I have previously noted that the doctrines of the church must be apostolic in origin. These are contained in the twenty-seven books comprising the New Testament.[54]

---

53 Walker: 57.
54 See John 20:30-31; 2 Timothy 3:16–17; 1 Corinthians 14:37; and 2 Peter 1:2–3.

NOTES

The doctrinal apostasy from the New Testament, for the most part, was contemporaneous with the rise in the power and importance of the general councils. Since the eighth century AD, it has largely been a matter of defining and perfecting innovations brought in during the period from AD 250 to AD 787.

What one accepts as doctrine will depend upon his/her concept of authority.[55] God, who is the source of all authority, delegated authority to Christ, who in turn commissioned the apostles, who through the Holy Spirit were guided into all truth.[56] The apostles, through the New Testament, continue to exercise that delegated authority in the heart of every Christian.

The Roman Catholic concept of authority was first defined by Cyprian, Bishop of Carthage. He taught that the bishop represents Christ in his congregation, and that the sum total of bishops, i.e., the ecumenical or general council, can legislate for the whole church. By this means the "infallibility" of the church was established, displacing the infallibility of the apostolic testimony.

We have already studied some of the doctrinal departures from the "faith which was once for all handed down to the saints" (Jude 3). It would be far beyond the scope of this study to trace historically every false doctrine that men have held. However, I feel that it is indispensable to a proper understanding of subsequent studies to note the following departures.

1. Baptism. The apostolic practice was to immerse penitent believers in order to have their sins forgiven.[57] With the apostasy came the practice of baptizing infants. The first mention of such a practice was by Irenaeus in the latter half of the second century AD: "He [Jesus] came to redeem all by himself; all who through him are *regenerated* to God, *infants*, little children, boys, young men and old."[58] It is assumed that "regenerated" refers to baptism.

The first writer to expressly mention the practice of infant baptism is Tertullian (AD 160–250). But he mentions it only to condemn it:

> The delay of baptism is preferable; principally, however in the case of little children. . . . Let them "come," while they are growing up; let them "come" while they are learning whither to come; let them become Christians when they are able to know Christ. More caution will be exercised in worldly matters: so that one who is not trusted with earthly substance is trusted with divine! Let them know how

55 For an excellent sermon on the subject "Authority in Christianity," read the one by John T. Smithson, Jr., in the Abilene Christian College Lectures. (Austin, TX: Firm Foundation Publishing Company, 1960), 27–43.
56 John 16:13; 14:25-26; Matthew 10:16–20.
57 Acts 2:38; 22:16; Romans 6:3–4.
58 Irenaeus, *Against Heresies.* Book II, Chapter 22, Sec. 4.

to "ask" for salvation, that you may seem (at least) to have given "to him that asketh."[59]

Origen lived at the same time as Tertullian. He was the first to advocate the baptism of infants. He claimed that this was an apostolic practice, although he did not produce any evidence to support his claim. He said, "None is free from pollution, though his life be but the length of one ray upon the earth. And it is for that reason, because the sacrament of baptism that pollution of our birth is taken away, that infants are baptized."[60]

Henry Alford, the great English exegete of the Scriptures, contrary to the practice of his denomination—the church of England—decisively states:

> The language of the Bible is against them; and, on their own ground, this is a very sore perplexity. There is one escape, and that a perfectly effectual one; but they are unwilling to avail themselves of its assistance. They might declare, and they ought to declare, that infant baptism was a practice unknown to the apostles; that not only does the New Testament not give one single expression which plainly and necessarily implies that infants were baptized in the apostolic churches but it can be fairly argued from a passage in chap. vii of I Corinthians that such a practice could not have existed at Corinth.[61]

Another apostasy in the doctrine of baptism was the substitution of sprinkling and pouring for immersion.[62] The first example of sprinkling instead of immersion is from the third century AD. A certain Novatus (Novatian) was seriously ill and while in bed, he received affusion. Eusebius, a church historian who lived in that century, gives us a description of the act:

> He ... when attacked with an obstinate disease, and being supposed at the point of death, was baptized by aspersion, in the bed on which he lay; if, indeed, it be proper to say that one like him received baptism. . . . This illustrious character abandoning the church of God, in which, when he was converted he was honoured with the presbytery, and that by favour of the bishop placing his hands upon him, to the order of bishops, and as all the clergy and many of the laity resisted it, since it was not lawful that one baptized in his sick bed by aspersion, as he was, should be promoted to any order of the clergy.[63]

---

59 Tertullian, *On Baptism.* Chapter XVIII.
60 Origen, *Works,* Vol. I:65.
61 Henry Alford, *Contemporary Review,* Vol. X, March, 1869: 329.
62 Our English word "baptize" is a transliteration of the Greek word βαπτίζω, *baptidzo* which means "dip, immerse." Ardnt and Gingrich: 131; Abbot-Smith: 74.
63 Eusebius, *Ecclesiastical History.* (Grand Rapids: Baker Book House, 1958), Book VI, Chapter XLIII, p. 266.

NOTES

The practice that was accepted by some and rejected by others, as is evidenced in the above statement, was called "clinical baptism." Everett Ferguson states that "affusion was slow in winning favor and continued to be confined to cases of emergency, being the exception as late as the ninth century."[64] He also states:

> The theology of baptism presented in the New Testament would seem to rule out infant baptism, in spite of its long history in Catholic and Protestant churches. Against the practice are the following facts.(1) There is no mention of the baptism of infants in the New Testament.(2) Every account of baptism in the New Testament shows it to be response by believers (cf. Acts 18:8 as representative). (3) The evidence of church history places the beginning of infant baptism at the end of the second century.[65]

The general acceptance of sprinkling came at a much later date. It was sanctioned by Pope Stephen III:

> The first law for sprinkling was obtained in the following manner. Pope Stephen III, being driven from Rome by Astulphus, king of the Lombards, in 753, fled to Pepin, who a short time before had usurped the crown of France. Whilst he remained there, the monks of Cressy in Brittany consulted him, whether, in case of necessity, baptism performed by pouring water on the head of the infant, be lawful. Stephen replied that it would. It was not till 1311, that the legislature in a council held at Ravenna, declared immersion or sprinkling to be indifferent.[66]

2. Penance and Indulgences. The Sacrament of Penance and the sell of indulgences are doctrinally connected in Roman Catholic theology. They are worthy of our consideration because of the important effects that they had in later church history. Philip Schaff said: "The Sacrament of Penance and priestly absolution included three elements: contrition of the heart, confession by the mouth, satisfaction by good works. On these conditions the priest grants absolution, not simply by a declaratory but by a judicial act."[67] He continues: "The idea of repentance was externalized and identified with certain outward acts of self-abasement or self-punishment for the expiation of sin. The public penance before the church went out of use during the seventh or eighth century except for very gross offences and was replaced by private penance and confession."[68]

The practice of penance is a corruption of the biblical practice of confession of sins. In apostolic times, the Christians who

---

64 Everett, Ferguson, "Baptism from the Second to the Fourth Century," in *The Restoration Quarterly*. Vol. 1, No. 4: 194.
65 Ferguson, *The Church of Christ*: 195–196.
66 *Edinburgh Cyclopedia,* s.v. "Baptism," Vol. II:245.
67 Schaff: IV, 382.
68 Ibid.

sinned would confess to their fellow Christians (not to a priest): "Therefore, confess your sins to one another, and pray for one another so that you may be healed. The effective prayer of a righteous man can accomplish much" (James 5:16). The apostle John said, "If we confess our sins, He is faithful and righteous to forgive us our sins and to cleanse us from all unrighteousness" (1 John 1:9). The New Testament illustrates the practice of confession of sins to fellow Christians.

The doctrine of a priest hearing confession came with the rise of Roman Catholicism, and is foreign to the tenor of the New Testament. The Catholic Encyclopedia describes the doctrine now held by that church:

> The institution of confession was necessary in order that the sin of the penitent might be revealed to Christ's minister; hence, the minister to whom the confession is made must have judicial power as representing Christ, the Judge of the living and the dead. This power again requires two things: authority of knowledge and power to absolve or to condemn.[69]

> Confession is the avowal of one's own sins made to a duly authorized priest for the purpose of obtaining their forgiveness through the power of the keys . . . called auricular, i.e., spoken into the ear of the confessor.[70]

Confession as practiced in the Roman Catholic Church today received official sanction at the Lateran Council in AD 1215. A decree of that council declared "the church has always understood that an entire confession of sins was always appointed by the Lord, and that it is of divine requirement necessary to all who have lapsed."[71] This same council further prescribed the necessity of confession as an article of belief, and gave as the law to the minimum frequency of confession as at least once a year.[72]

The sale of indulgences rose out of the sacrament of Penance. Mosheim credits Thomas Aquinas, the great Roman Catholic theologian of the thirteenth century, with the formulation of the idea of selling indulgences:

> That there actually existed an immense treasure of *merit* composed of the pious deeds, and the virtuous actions, which the saints had performed *beyond what was necessary* for their own salvation, and which were therefore applicable to the benefit of others; that the guardian and dispenser of this precious treasure was the Roman pontiff; and that of consequence he was empowered to

69 *Catholic Encyclopedia.* Vol. XI: 626.
70 Ibid.: 625.
71 Quoted in: J. W. Shepherd, *The Church, the Falling Away, and the Restoration.* (Nashville: The Gospel Advocate Company, 1954), 64.
72 *Catholic Encyclopedia.* Vol. XI: 626.

NOTES

assign such as he thought proper, a portion of this inexhaustible source of *merit*, suitable to their respective guilt, and sufficient to deliver them for the punishment due their crimes.[73]

An indulgence is defined officially as "the extra-sacramental remission of the temporal punishment due, in God's justice, to sin that has been forgiven, which remission is granted by the Church in the exercise of the power of the keys, through the application of the superabundant merits of Christ and of the saints, and for some just and reasonable motive."[74]

The Popes came to see in the sale of indulgences a source of great wealth. Gregory VI, in AD 1046, promised them to all who sent contributions for the repair of churches in Rome.[75] The gross abuses of this shameful traffic in merits culminated under Leo X, who employed John Tetzel to sell indulgences for the "holy" purpose of enlarging and furnishing St. Peter's Basilica in Rome. Tetzel, a Dominican monk, was an eloquent preacher and a super salesman. In his sermons, he would dwell on the flames and torments of purgatory, and of those dear friends and loved ones who were at that very moment crying to their families and friends to help loose them from the torments of that place. Concluding his sermon, he would rush over to the indulgence box and begin to take contributions for the liberation of souls from torment.

This appalling state of affairs in the Roman Catholic Church was one of the primary reasons for the Protestant Reformation, which most historians date from Martin Luther's nailing of his ninety-five theses protesting the sale of indulgences to the door of the All-Saints Church in Wittenberg, Germany in AD 1517.[76]

Points to Ponder

1. The term "catholic" means (a. righteous; b. universal; c. church).
2. The doctrinal apostasies that resulted in the Roman Catholic church were contemporaneous with the rise in power of (a. the Roman Emperors; b. the general councils; c. the Popes).
3. The Roman Catholic Church accepts as authoritative (a. only the Bible; b. the Bible and the decisions of councils and popes).

73 Mosheim: I, 294.
74 *Catholic Encyclopedia.* Vol. XI, 626.
75 Ibid., Vol. VII, 783.
76 For an example of the modern use of indulgences in the Roman Catholic Church, read the excellent article written by my friend Keith Robinson while he was an evangelist in Rome, Italy: Appendix C.

4. The sprinkling of infants (a. was; b. was not) practiced by the apostles of Christ.

5. The first person to advocate baptism of infants was (a. Tertullian; b. Origen).

6. The first example of sprinkling or pouring instead of immersion occurred in the (a. second; b. third; c. sixth) century AD.

7. The first example of sprinkling or pouring was called (a. infant baptism; b. clinical baptism)

Now Let's Review

(Answer these true-false statements without looking at the material that you have studied, then turn back and review the material to see how many you answered correctly.)

_____ 1. The apostles of Christ forewarned the church of the coming apostasy.

_____ 2. The office of "president" of the presbytery (eldership) was apostolic in origin.

_____ 3. The distinction between "presbyters" and "bishops" was firmly established by the time of Cyprian.

_____ 4. Gregory the Great was the first to use the title "universal bishop."

_____ 5. John the Faster denounced Gregory for usurping the title "universal bishop."

_____ 6. The dispute over pre-eminence brought about the split between Greek and Roman Catholics.

_____ 7. The first general council was held at Nicea in AD 325.

_____ 8. Most of the apostasies in church government were affected by the fourth century.

_____ 9. The apostasies in worship were "to bring it up to date."

_____ 10. Emperor Trajan was mainly responsible for secularizing the church.

_____ 11. The Catholic doctrine of the literal sacrifice of Christ each time the Lord's Supper is observed is called "transubstantiation."

_____ 12. Pope Vitalian is recognized as introducing instrumental music into worship.

_____ 13. The veneration (worship) of saints dates to the second century AD.

NOTES

_____ 14. Religious relics in Catholic doctrine can only be physical parts of saints.

_____ 15. Christians in the first century AD celebrated the 25th of December as the anniversary of Jesus' birth.

_____ 16. Baptism of infants began in the second century AD.

_____ 17. Sprinkling, instead of immersion, gained official sanction in the Roman Catholic Church in AD 1311.

_____ 18. Sprinkling was referred to as "clinical baptism" when it was first practiced.

_____ 19. An "indulgence" in Roman Catholic doctrine is a license to sin.

_____ 20. Most historians date the beginning of the Protestant Reformation to AD 1517.

Part III

The Reformation That Resulted in Protestant Denominationalism

Roman Catholicism held the western world in her iron grip for nearly a thousand years, from the sixth through the sixteenth centuries AD. This period has been called the "Dark Ages"[1] of church history and, as it applies to the New Testament church, it is not a misnomer! The countless apostasies introduced into the government, doctrine, and worship of the church served to render Christianity ineffectual to carry out the purposes intended by our Lord.

The Reformation, beginning in the sixteenth century AD,[2] represented an effort on the part of sincere men to bring about a reform *within* the framework of the Roman Catholic Church. When their attempts at reform were repulsed by the Catholic hierarchy; they separated themselves from the Roman Catholic Church to form "protesting" groups—each with its own form of government and system of doctrines.

A Early Attempts at Reform

It would be beyond the scope of this study to examine all of the attempts made by sincere and honest people to reform some facet of the doctrine or practice of the Roman Catholic Church. Some of these who carried out reforms within the framework of that system while accepting the overall prerogative of the Roman Catholic Church are noted below.

1. Claudius of Turin (d. AD 839). The ninth century AD was noted as the period of the great Greek iconoclasts (image breakers). This was a reaction against the use of images and prostrating oneself before them. In the Roman church, Claudius, who became Bishop of Turin, Italy in AD 823, ordered that all images be cast out of the churches and burned. He denied that the cross was to be honored with any kind of worship. He treated relics with contempt, declaring that they had absolutely no

---

1 Kenneth Scott Latourette, a noted church historian, in his seven volume history of Christianity, entitled volume two written on this period: "The Thousand Years of Uncertainty." Kenneth Scott Latourette, *A History of the Expansion of Christianity*. 7 vols. (Grand Rapids, MI: Zondervan Publishing House, 1970).

2 Actually, as we shall see in "Early Attempts at Reform," sincere men and women were disturbed by apostasies much earlier than the sixteenth century AD.

NOTES

merit in God's sight. Mosheim writes that "hence it happened that the city of Turin and the adjacent country were, for a long time after the death of Claudius, much less infected with superstition than the other parts of Europe.[3]

2. Peter of Bruys (d. AD 1135). Peter of Bruys lived in southern France in the twelfth century AD. He is described as a fervent preacher, bordering on radicalism. He combined a strict asceticism with denial of several cardinal Catholic doctrines: infant baptism, the mass, instrumental music, ceremonies and prayers for the dead. The church imprisoned him and eventually a mob burned him at the stake for heresy.[4]

3. Peter Waldo (or Valdez) (d. AD 1218). Peter Waldo was a rich merchant of Lyons, France. He gave away his estate to follow literally the words of Christ: "If you wish to be complete, go and sell your possessions and give to the poor, and you will have treasure in heaven; and come, follow Me" (Matt. 19:21). His example had a marked effect upon his friends. He was soon followed by others who called themselves the "poor in spirit."

In order to know his duty toward God more perfectly, Waldo procured a translation of the New Testament. He went from city to city preaching this new-found faith. In AD 1179, Waldo and his followers appealed to the Third Lateran Council for permission to preach. Although neither this Council nor Pope Alexander III considered them heretical, they were refused permission to preach on the grounds of being "ignorant laymen." Waldo regarded this refusal as the voice of man (the Pope) against the voice of God. The Waldensians became more fervent in their preaching. In AD 1184, Pope Lucius III, after repeated attempts to silence them, excommunicated them for their disobedience.[5]

In the nineteenth century, Pope Innocent VIII branded the Waldensians as "venomous serpents" and urged the King of France to proceed against them with armed expeditions to exterminate them.[6]

Distinguishing characteristics of the Waldensians were: (1) The principle that the Bible, especially the New Testament, is the sole rule of belief and life. (2) Secret prayer was deemed a valuable aid to piety. (3) Abandonment of the complicated and corrupt organization and elaborate ritual of the Roman Catholic Church.[7] The Waldensian Church is still in existence in France and Italy.

3 Mosheim: I, 204.
4 See: Walker, 1959: 227 and Latourette, Expansion: 2: 432.
5 Walker, 1959: 229.
6 Jacobs: 146.
7 Schaff: VII, 513.

4. William of Occam (AD 1280–1339). William was an English Franciscan monk of great learning. Williston Walker lists his contribution as, defending "the independence of the state from ecclesiastical authority." He also taught that Scripture and not the decisions of councils and popes is alone binding on Christians.[8]

5. John Wickliff (Wyclif)—(AD 1328–1384). John Wickliff was born in Yorkshire, England. He has been called the "Morning Star of the Reformation" because of his contributions toward reforming the church. His greatest contribution was seen in his appreciation for the Scriptures and his desire that they be known by "every plow-boy in England." Walker notes:

> The Scriptures, he taught, are the only law of the church. . . . Convinced that the Bible is the law of God, Wyclif determined to give it to the people in the English tongue. Between 1382–1384, the Scriptures were translated from the Vulgate. . . . It has been usually thought that the New Testament was from his pen, and the Old Testament from that of Nicholas of Hereford.[9]

Wickliff further held that preaching was to be exalted; the papacy was non-essential to the being of the Church; that the church is the congregation of the elect; that priestly absolution and transubstantiation are not biblical and that marriage on biblical grounds is honorable for all men.[10]

The beliefs of Wickliff caused the Pope to heap abuse and anathemas upon him. However, due to the esteem which he enjoyed in the court of England, it was impossible for the Pope to inflict bodily injury upon him. After his death, when circumstances were more favorable in England for the papal forces, his mortal remains were exhumed, placed on a chair, tried, sentenced to burn at the stake, then his ashes were thrown into the River Swift. At this same time [AD 1414], the Roman Catholic church condemned the reading of the Bible translated by Wickliff, upon the pain of "forfeiture of land, cattle, life, and goods from their heirs forever."[11]

6. John Huss (AD 1373–1415). John Huss, a Bohemian, lived contemporaneously with the latter portion of Wickliff's life. It was in Huss that Wickliff found his most ardent disciple. Wickliff's greatest influence was not in his native England but at Prague among the "Bohemian Brethren."

Huss was born to a poor peasant family in Husinecz (Czechoslovakia). He was educated at the University of Prague,

---

8 Walker, 1959: 251–252.
9 Walker, 1959: 269.
10 Schaff: VIII, 346.
11 Schaff: VIII, 344.

NOTES

receiving his Master of Arts degree in AD 1396. In AD 1401 he was ordained to the priesthood and became rector of the University in 1402. Huss, following the lead of Wickliff, insisted upon preaching as the right of every priest. He urged moral reform among the citizens of Prague. His open rebellion against Pope John XXIII in AD 1411 was brought on by the sale of indulgences:

> John XXIII called Europe to a crusade against Ladislaus of Naples, the defender of Gregory XII, and promised indulgences to all participating in it, whether by personal enlistment or by gifts. Wenzel Tiem, dean of Passau, appointed preacher of the Holy War, made his way to Prague and opened the sale of indulgences. Chests were placed in the great churches, and the traffic was soon in full sway.[12]

Walker notes that Huss opposed, holding that the Pope had no right to use physical force, that money payments effected no true forgiveness, and unless of the predestinate, the indulgence could be of no value to a man.[13]

Because of his opposition, Huss was excommunicated by the Pope and ordered to appear before the Council of Constance. The Roman Emperor urged Huss to go to Constance promising him a "safe-conduct." However, upon his arrival there, he was unceremoniously cast into prison where he languished for seven months. On Saturday, July 6, 1415, Huss was conducted to the cathedral of Constance. The following is an account of the proceedings against him:

> It was 6 AM and he [Huss] was kept waiting outside the doors until the celebration of the mass was completed. He was then admitted to the sacred edifice, but not to make a defense, as he had come to Constance hoping to do. He was to listen to sentence pronounced upon him as an ecclesiastical outcast and criminal. He was placed in the middle of the church on a high stool, set there specially for him. The bishop of Lodi preached from Rom. 6:6, "That the body of sin might be destroyed." The extermination of heretics was represented as one of the works most pleasing to God, and the preacher used the time-worn illustration from the rotten piece of flesh, the little spark which is in danger of turning into a great flame and the creeping cancer. The most virulent the poison the swifter should be the application of the cauterizing iron.[14]

He was then taken out of the cathedral and burned at a stake set up in the space before the church.

7. Jerome Savonarola (AD 1452–1498). Philip Schaff described Savonarola as the "most imposing preacher of the Middle Ages and one of the most noteworthy preachers of righteousness since

---

12 Ibid., 364.
13 Walker, 1959: 272.
14 Schaff: VII, 380–381.

St. Paul."[15] He was born at Ferrara, Italy. His father was a physician. He had hoped that his son would follow him in the practice of medicine. However, several reasons combined to cause him to leave his home to go to Bologna at the age of 23 where he entered the Dominican monastic order. He wrote a letter to his father explaining the reason for his abrupt departure: "I could not endure any longer the wickedness of the blinded peoples of Italy. Virtue I saw despised everywhere, the vices exalted and held in honor."[16]

In AD 1491, he came to Florence and soon distinguished himself as a great disclaimer against the moral degeneration of his day. Within five years, he was virtual ruler of the city. Vast numbers flocked to hear him preach, attesting to his popularity. He considered himself a messenger appointed by God to announce judgment upon the iniquities of the people. He gave himself ardently to the task.

Papal opposition to Savonarola came about more from political than religious reasons. He denounced the misrule of the Pope. In turn, the Pope excommunicated him and demanded that he be punished. In April 1498 he was arrested and tortured. A month later, on May 23rd, he was hanged and his body burned. His ashes were thrown into the Arno River that flows through the city of Florence.

8. John Reuchlin (AD 1455–1522) and Erasmus (AD 1465–1536). Though not properly religious leaders, these two imminent scholars should be mentioned for the influence that their high literary achievement had upon the Reformation Movement.

Reuchlin was trained as a lawyer but also became a noted linguist. His first important work was a Latin lexicon. His chief contribution was as a pioneer in the restoring of knowledge of the Hebrew language. He gave a scientific basis for the study of this language in his Hebrew grammar and dictionary which was published in AD 1506. He was the uncle of Philip Melanchthon—friend of Martin Luther—whom he recommended as professor of Greek in the University of Wittenberg, Germany.

Erasmus of Rotterdam was well known for his Greek scholarship. He established the Greek pronunciation that goes by his name; edited and translated Greek classics; and, translated the writings of the "church fathers." Erasmus issued the first printed Greek New Testament and advocated its translation into the languages spoken in his day.

15 Schaff: VII, 686
16 Ibid.

NOTES

Points to Ponder

1. The period known as the "Dark Ages" covers (a. 500 years; b. 750 years; c. 1000 years).
2. Place the letter for the name of the man which the description fits:
   _____ Claudius of Turin
   _____ Peter of Bruys
   _____ Peter Waldo
   _____ William of Occam
   _____ John Wickliff
   _____ John Huss
   _____ Jerome Savonarola
   _____ Erasmus

   a. "Morning Star of the Reformation"
   b. French ascetic of the 12th century
   c. Hebrew scholar
   d. 9th century Roman iconoclast
   e. Greek scholar
   f. Rich merchant who became a poor preacher
   g. Founder of the Bohemian Brethren
   h. Defended the separation of Church and State

B. Immediate Causes of the Protestant Reformation of the Sixteenth Century
   Some of the reasons giving rise to the Protestant Reformation in Europe are:[17]
   1. The tyrannical disposition of the Popes during the middle ages. They had prostituted spiritual things to their own personal benefit. Even the choice of who would be Pope depended largely upon political favoritism and nepotism. Some Popes were killed so that others might occupy the "chair of Peter." At one time, three different men claimed to be Pope at the same time. Each one pronounced anathemas upon the other two. Some of the most licentious men imaginable were occupying the papacy. "Alexander VI was referred to as a 'Papal Nero,' destitute of all religious virtues and principles."[18] Julian II was a politician and warrior. Leo X had far more interest in the revival of pagan literature and art than he did in religion. It is even thought by some that he was an atheist.
   2. The cardinals, bishops, priests, and monks followed the example of their "chief shepherd" by entering into great immoralities. Literature of this period is full of complaints and exposures of

---

17 For a full discussion of these reasons consult: Schaff; VII, 8ff.
18 Mosheim: I, 387.

the ignorance, vulgarity, and immorality of the priests. Simony and nepotism were widely practiced.

3. Religious discipline in the churches was destroyed because of the flagrant violations of spiritual laws by those who pretended to be spiritual leaders.

4. The study of the Scriptures was abandoned. Carlstadt, the older colleague of Luther, confessed that he had been made a "Doctor of Divinity" before he had even seen a complete copy of the Bible—much less studied it!

5. Preaching was neglected or used to the ignominious ends of promoting the sale of indulgences.

6. Endless rites, ceremonies, and image worship obstructed true worship to God.

7. Meritorious works were substituted for good works.

8. Remission of sins could be bought with money. The sale of indulgences was carried on under the direction of the Pope.

9. The rise of Scholasticism and the renewal of the desire for learning among the "laity" caused a greater respect for the Scriptures as authority in faith and morals.

10. Many European kings and princes favored the full separation of church from the state.

C. Fundamental Principles of the Protestant Reformation Movement
The principles listed below were held by different men in different degrees, but they are all characteristic of the Protestant Reformation.

1. The Bible was accepted as the only infallible rule of faith and practice. This was in opposition to the Roman Catholic doctrine that Scripture and ecclesiastical tradition are both to be accepted as a rule of faith.

2. Luther stated one of the principles which has remained as an important one in Protestant groups: "What is not contrary to Scripture is for Scripture and Scripture for it."[19] It states simply that anything may be accepted in religion *that does not expressly contradict the Scriptures.* It is a negative approach to the Bible. Such things as sprinkling of babies and the use of instrumental music were brought into Protestant churches by the use of this principle. Both have as their only authority the Roman Catholic Church!

3. The doctrine of justification by faith alone (Luther's *sola fide*) as distinct from the Catholic doctrine of justification by faith and works of human merit.

4. The principle of the "priesthood of all believers" as contrasted to the special Roman Catholic priesthood.

---

19 Walker: 314.

NOTES

5. Removal of obstructions between the believer and Christ; such as, intercession of saints and Mary.

Points to Ponder

1. The Popes of the Middle Ages were known for their (a. virtues; b. vices).
2. (a. Pope Pius X; b. Leo X; c. Alexander VI) is considered by many church historians to have been an atheist.
3. Preaching was (a. prominent; b. neglected) in the Catholic church during the Middle Ages.
4. Yes or No? The Roman Catholic Church favors the separation of church and state.
5. The Reformers accepted only the authority of (a. tradition; b. Scripture).
6. The Reformers adopted a (a. positive; b. negative) approach to the authority of Scripture.
7. Luther believed in justification by (a. faith plus meritorious works; b. faith alone).

D. Brief Study of the Lives and Doctrines of the Reform Leaders
   1. Martin Luther (AD 1483–1546)

Luther was born in Eisleben, Germany; the son of a poor peasant miner. He was reared in an atmosphere of simple, strict piety. His parents being Catholics; he received instruction in that religion but no biblical instruction.

The sudden death of a close friend caused him to break off the study of law to enter a monastery of Augustinian hermits in Erfurt in 1505. In 1507, he was ordained to the priesthood of the Roman Catholic Church. The next year he was sent by his superiors to Wittenberg to study in preparation for a future professorship at the University that had been established by Frederick III, Elector of Saxony. Frederick became a staunch friend and protector of Luther. Luther was awarded the Doctor of Theology degree in 1512. He began, at once, to lecture on the Bible. He taught Psalms, Romans, Galatians, Hebrews, and Titus.

Luther felt a deep sense of his own sinfulness and his first deviation from the Roman Catholic Church was in believing that salvation is a new relation to God, not based on works of merit, but on absolute trust or faith in God.

Shortly after beginning his professorship, Luther made a trip to Rome. He was greatly disappointed by what he witnessed in the "holy city." In AD 1517, Luther spoke out against one of the greatest abuses: the sale of indulgences.

Pope Leo X sold the archbishopric of Mainz, Germany to Albrecht upon the condition of payment of a large sum of money.

To raise this money Albrecht secured, as his share, half of the proceeds from the sale of indulgences in the district. The papacy was raising money to build the new basilica, St. Peter's Cathedral in Rome. Johann Tetzel was commissioned to sell indulgences. He has been described as an unscrupulous, super-salesman. Luther influenced Frederick III to not allow Tetzel to enter Saxony. He further preached on the abuse of indulgences. On October 31, 1517, he nailed his famous ninety-five theses against the sale of indulgences to the door of All Saints Church in Wittenberg. It was a common practice to place notices for discussion on church doors.

Tetzel replied at once and stirred up others to come to his defense against Luther. Johann Maier of Eck, professor of theology in the University of Ingolstadt, was one of Luther's most formidable opponents. He branded Luther as a heretic. By the beginning of AD 1518, complaints against Luther had been issued at Rome. The Augustinian Vicar General was ordered to end the dispute. However, Luther argued with such skill that he won new friends to his cause. He was ordered to appear in Rome in 1518 but wisely refused to go. Eck influenced the Pope to issue a papal bull of condemnation which was published on June 15, 1520. Luther's reply was to publicly burn it in the presence of the students and townspeople of Wittenberg.

Luther was summoned to Worms under the protection of an imperial safe-conduct. As he traveled from Wittenberg to Worms, he was well received in every city as a hero of those who opposed the abuses in the sale of indulgences. On April 17, 1521, he appeared before the Emperor and was asked to recant. He replied with his famous statement that unless he was shown from the Scripture the falsehood of his arguments he could not recant: "I cannot do otherwise. Here I stand. God help me, Amen."[20]

As Luther was leaving Worms to return to Wittenberg, Elector Frederick had him seized by friends and spirited away to Wartburg Castle, near Eisenach. Frederick is credited with saving Luther's life from the conspirators who were seeking to silence him. Luther remained in hiding for months. It was during this enforced retirement that Luther made one of his most lasting contributions by translating the New Testament into the German language.

Late in AD 1522 the first protestant congregations were formed. Luther gave to these a constitution and fixed order of services. The Lutheran churches today are an outgrowth of this movement. Luther prepared a catechism in 1529, of which,

---

20 Quoted in Walker, 1959: 310.

NOTES

Walker declares, the "Short Catechism is one of the noblest monuments of the reformation."[21]

2. Philip Melanchthon (AD 1497–1560)

Melanchthon was born at Bretten, Germany to a noble family. His mother was the niece of the famous Hebrew scholar Reuchlin whom we have previously mentioned. Reuchlin presented Melanchthon with a Bible at an early age and directed his studies. He received his Master of Arts degree in 1514 at the age of seventeen. His literary brilliance was already apparent at that age.

Reuchlin, a friend of Elector Frederick, recommended Melanchthon to the University of Wittenberg. He began teaching there in August 1518—only ten months after Luther had nailed his Theses to the church door. In the same year, Melanchthon published a Greek grammar that enjoyed wide success. He became a popular teacher. Students came from all over Europe to attend his lectures.

His academic training and his knowledge of the Bible naturally inclined him to the evangelical movement of Luther. They became fast friends. He said of Luther, "I would rather die than be separated from him."[22] The feeling was mutual for Luther wrote:

> I am rough, boisterous, stormy, and altogether warlike. I am born to fight against innumerable monsters and devils. I must remove stumps and stones, cut away thistles and thorns, and clear the wild forests; but Master Philippus comes along softly and gently sowing and watering with joy, according to the gifts which God has abundantly bestowed upon him.[23]

No doubt Luther and Melanchthon complimented and completed each other's work. Melanchthon has been acclaimed the "teacher of Germany."[24] He authored "The Augsburg Confession," a famous document stating the doctrinal basis of the Lutheran Church in Germany. The historian Philip Schaff says, "Without Luther the Reformation would never have taken hold of the common people; without Melanchthon it would never have succeeded among the scholars of Germany."[25]

3. Ulrich Zwingli (AD 1482–1531)

Zwingli was chief of the reformers of German-speaking Switzerland. He was born in Wildhaus, Switzerland. His father was chief magistrate of the village and his mother was the sister of a priest.

---

21 Walker, 1959: 319.
22 Schaff: VII, 192.
23 Ibid., 193.
24 Ibid., 195.
25 Ibid.

Zwingli became a preacher at Zurich on December 23, 1518. In January of the following year, he began a homiletical exposition of the New Testament in his sermons. To preach from the Scriptures was an innovation in his day! He continued this exposition for four years. In August 1518, Bernhardin Samson, a Franciscan monk of Milan, Italy, came to Switzerland to sell indulgences. Due to Zwingli's influence, he was not permitted to enter Zurich.

In 1522, Zwingli began his most vigorous reforms that included: (1) The sole authority of the Scriptures; (2) Salvation by faith alone; (3) Denial of the sacrificial quality of the mass and of saintly intercessions; (4) Recognition of Christ as the sole head of the church; (5) Allowing the clergy to marry; (6) Abolishing images, relics and organs from places of worship; (7) Making the sermon the center of the services; and, (8) The observance of the Lord's Supper as a symbolic or memorial supper.[26]

The five Roman Catholic cantons of Switzerland formed a political alliance with Ferdinand of Austria and marched against the Protestants of Zurich. Zwingli, who served as a chaplain to the army, was killed during the battles.

4. John Calvin (AD 1509–1564)

Calvin was born in Noyon, France. His father held a secure post in government and secured a liberal education for his son. Calvin attended the University of Paris and later studied law at the University of Orleans.

He was a devout student of the Bible and had been influenced somewhat by the reform writings of Luther and Melanchthon. He became a leader of the Paris Protestants, but because of the King's opposition he was forced to flee to Switzerland. He settled in Geneva where he became a powerful reformer.

At the age of 27, he published his famous *Institutes on the Christian Religion*. He was convinced of the absolute authority of the Scriptures and the doctrines of unconditional predestination and hereditary depravity. He is credited with introducing congregational singing into the worship of the Reform Church of Geneva. By the time of his death on May 26, 1564, he had greatly influence Geneva and other cities of Switzerland and France by his powerful preaching and by his writings.

5. Henry VIII (AD 1491–1544)

Henry VIII, King of England, could not be thought of as a religious reformer in the strictest sense. He was not a religious man. However, his desire to divorce Catherine of Aragon in

---

26 See: Walker, 1959: 322–325.

order to marry Anne Boleyn caused an open rupture between England and the Roman Catholic Church.

Paradoxically, in 1521, Pope Leo X had given Henry VIII the title "Defender of the Faith" for his defense of the sacraments against Luther's writings. Historians have described Henry VIII as "a tyrant under legal forms who was skilled in the administration of the affairs of the kingdom, but obstinate, egotistic and self-seeking in the furtherance of his own personal ends."[27]

The church formed after the separation from Rome was the Church of England (the Episcopal Church in America). The head of the Church of England is the king (or queen) who is currently reigning. Its doctrines and worship differ very little from those of the Roman Catholic Church.

6. John Knox (AD 1505—1572)

Knox was born in Haddington, Scotland. His early career is obscure but undoubtedly he was ordained into the priesthood of the Roman Catholic Church. He is first mentioned as a friend of Wishart, a Protestant who led in revolt against the papal forces of Scotland. Wishart was captured and burned at the stake by Cardinal Beaton on March 2, 1546. Knox was also taken prisoner and for the next nineteen months suffered the cruel lot of a galley-slave to the navy. Upon his release, he went to England and was appointed as one of the royal chaplains of Edward VI. However, when Queen Mary came to the throne, he was compelled to flee to Germany. Later he went to Geneva where he became an ardent disciple and friend of John Calvin. While in Geneva he worked on the Genevan version of the English Bible that was highly valued by English Puritans.

Knox returned to Scotland in 1559 to become the great reformer of Scotland and the founder of the Presbyterian Church. Its doctrines were greatly influenced by John Calvin. It became the state religion in 1560. Knox's death on November 24, 1572 marked the end of a fiery career that "influenced not merely the religion but the character of the nation more than any other man in Scottish history."[28]

Conclusion

The reformation movement had the salutary effect of curtailing the power and influence of Roman Catholicism. But it did not result in a return to the doctrines and practices revealed in the New Testament. Instead of presenting to the world one united body, it resulted in the establishment of numerous bodies with different

---

27 Walker, 1959: 358.
28 Ibid., 1959: 373.

doctrines and practices. They are known as denominations.[29] Each one exalts its divergent and contradictory creeds.

Points to Ponder

Identify the person described below by placing the letter: L for Luther; M for Melanchthon; Z for Zwingli; C for Calvin; H for Henry VIII; and K for Knox.

_____ A German who led the Reformation by nailing his ninety-five theses to the church door of Wittenberg
_____ A great Swiss Reformer killed in battle
_____ A colleague of Luther known for his great learning
_____ The French Reformer who lived in Geneva, Switzerland for many years
_____ He desired to divorce his wife to marry Anne Boleyn
_____ The Reformer of Scotland
_____ Author of the "Augsburg Confession"
_____ One of the translators of the Geneva Bible
_____ The preacher of Zurich, Switzerland

1. The Dominican monk who came into Saxony to sell indulgences was (a. Eck; b. Luther; c. Tetzel).
2. (a. Knox; b. Zwingli; c. Melanchthon) was kin to the great German scholar Reuchlin.
3. The reformation movement (a. succeeded completely; b. succeeded partially) in breaking away from the doctrinal system of the Roman Catholic Church.

---

29 See Appendix D for a list of major denominations with the dates of their beginning, their founder and other vital statistics. Also consult: Frank S. Mead, *Handbook of Denominations in the United States*. 4th Ed. (Nashville, TN: Abingdon Press, 1965). Most sections of Mead's book were read and corrected by authorities in the denominations discussed.

NOTES

Now Let's Review

Answer these true-false statements without looking at the material. Then turn back to Part III to review the material to see how many you answered correctly.

_____ 1. Claudius of Turin destroyed images in the churches.

_____ 2. Peter of Bruys was burned at the stake for heresy.

_____ 3. Peter Waldo became a Roman Catholic preacher.

_____ 4. Waldo and his followers were commissioned to preach by Pope Alexander III.

_____ 5. William of Occam defended the independence of the state from ecclesiastical authority.

_____ 6. John Wickliff was called the "Morning Star of the Reformation."

_____ 7. Wickliff was a German teacher in the University of Wittenberg.

_____ 8. John Huss was burned at the stake for heresy.

_____ 9. Jerome Savonarola was known as the great preacher of Florence, Italy.

_____ 10. Reuchlin and Erasmus were known for their linguistic scholarship.

_____ 11. The Middle Ages was known as a period of great fervor for the study of the Bible.

_____ 12. Luther was the great leader of the German Reformation.

_____ 13. Zwingli was a leader in the Swiss Reformation.

_____ 14. The Reformation leaders believed in the authority of tradition in addition to that of Scripture.

_____ 15. John Calvin, a Frenchman, lived for many years at Geneva, Switzerland and led in the Reformation there.

_____ 16. A licentious king seeking a divorce caused a rupture between the Catholics in England and the Pope in Rome.

_____ 17. John Knox was the leader of the Scottish Reformation.

_____ 18. The Protestant Reformation resulted in the renunciation of all doctrines not found in the Bible.

Part IV

The Restoration Principles and New Testament Christianity

The end of the eighteenth century and the dawning of the nineteenth were characterized by intense spiritual fervor and a great revival in religion. This was especially true in the United States. Great camp meetings were the order of the day with thousands turning to a deeper study of the Bible in a climate of complete freedom of religious expression—something they had not enjoyed in Europe.

Good men in different parts of the country were beginning to ask questions and to ponder the seriousness of religious division that was so prevalent in their day. Carroll Ellis stated that there were twelve kinds of Presbyterian churches; thirteen different types of Baptist churches; and, seventeen different Methodist communions. None of them had fellowship with the others.[1]

All too frequently the shadows of Roman Catholicism could be seen in the doctrines and practices of existing denominations. The forms of church government in some reflected the hand of the Pope instead of the hand of God from the Bible. Many came to have a desire to "restore the ancient order of things" found in the New Testament.

James M. Tolle said: "They saw what the reformers had failed to see: the all-important truth that what the world needed was not a reformation of apostate religion but a complete, full return to the purity of the first century church. . . . Their work was expressly a work of restoration."[2]

A. Four Basic Principles of the Restoration Movement
   1. The acknowledgement of the New Testament Scriptures as the only authoritative rule of faith and practice for the Christian. A positive attempt to "contend earnestly for the faith which was once for all handed down to the saints" (Jude 3). They accepted only those things that are specifically *prescribed* in the New Testament by command, apostolic example or necessary inference.

---

1 Class notes in Restoration Preaching at David Lipscomb College, September 1955.
2 *The Church, Apostasy, Reformation, and Restoration* (phamplet): 22–23.

NOTES

2. Renunciation of all human creeds and the acceptance of the teaching of Jesus and the apostles as the only creed binding upon Christians. Human creeds are by their very nature divisive; only the Scriptures furnish a rational basis of unity.
3. The restoration of the New Testament concept of the church in the minds of men; worshipping and patterning our lives after the divine teaching.
4. The unity of all Christians upon the basis of the Bible.

Points to Ponder

1. What is the basic difference in the ideas of "reformation" and "restoration?"
2. Do you consider the four basic principles of restoration valid? Why?

B. Leaders in the Restoration of New Testament Principles of Christianity and Their Particular Contributions
   1. James O'Kelly (1757–1826)

   In 1792, a Methodist preacher named James O'Kelly, who labored in Virginia and North Carolina, led in one of the earliest known attempts at restoration of New Testament principles in North America. He, with four other Methodist preachers of Virginia, withdrew from that communion on November 1, 1794 because of the autocratic policies of Francis Asbury, the Methodist Episcopal Bishop at that time.

   They formed a body known as the "Republican Methodist Church." This new group met at Lebanon, Virginia in August 1795. It distinguished itself by attempting to go back to only New Testament principles. At the regular meeting, Rice Haggard, a member of the committee arose to tell the assembly that they were having difficulty formulating a creed. He said:

   > Brethren, this [holding aloft a Bible] is a sufficient rule of faith and practice. By it we are told that the disciples were called Christians and I move henceforth and forever that the followers of Christ be known as Christians simply.[3]

   Following Haggard's appeal, a brother Hafferty of North Carolina stood up and moved that they take the Bible itself as their only creed. From these two motions were devised what became known as the "Five Cardinal Principles:" (1) The Lord Jesus Christ as the only Head of the Church; (2) The name Christian to the exclusion of all party and sectarian names; (3) The Holy Bible, or the Scriptures of the Old and New

---

3 Earl Irvin West, *The Search for the Ancient Order.* 3 Vols. (Nashville, TN: Gospel Advocate Company, 1949), I: 10.

Testament our only creed, and a sufficient rule of faith and practice; (4) Christian character, or vital piety, the only test of church fellowship and membership; and, (5) The right of private judgment, and liberty of conscience, the privilege and duty of all.[4]

In 1801, the name "Republican Methodist" was discarded in favor of being known only as Christians. Although there were evident weaknesses, nevertheless, a beginning was being made to return to the principles of New Testament Christianity.

2. Elias Smith and Abner Jones

In Vermont, Abner Jones, a physician, became greatly dissatisfied with sectarian names and creeds. He began preaching among the Baptist churches that denominational membership and party distinctions should be abolished. In September, 1800, he succeeded in establishing a church at Lyndon, Vermont based upon restoration principles. Elias Smith, a Baptist preacher, soon joined him. Together they exhorted and preached with the result that several congregations discarded denominational creeds and called themselves Christians.[5] A significant factor to remember is that although the conclusions reached by the various men were strikingly similar, they worked without knowledge of one another.

3. Barton Warren Stone (1772–1844)

Barton Warren Stone was born at Port Tobacco Creek, Maryland on December 24, 1772. His father died when he was only three years old and his mother moved the family shortly thereafter into the Dan River country of North Carolina. One of the battles of the Civil War was fought at Guilford Courthouse, not far from the Stone family homestead.

The division of the family estate was made when Barton Stone was sixteen years old. He wisely decided to use his portion to obtain an education. He had decided to study jurisprudence to become a judge. Accordingly, he went to the famous school of David Caldwell in North Carolina.

The dominant influence in Caldwell's school was religion. This made Stone very uncomfortable as he had not joined any of the denominations near his home. James McGready, one of the popular Presbyterian preachers of North Carolina, was holding a revival near the school and about thirty of the students "got religion." Stone forced himself to avoid religious interest as he felt this would hinder his being a judge. He determined to leave Caldwell's school to attend Hampden-Sidney College

---

4 Ibid.

5 J. W. Shepherd, *The Church, the Falling Away, and the Restoration.* (Nashville, TN: The Gospel Advocate Company, 1954), 149.

NOTES

in Virginia. There was a violent storm the day he was scheduled to leave. He spent the day in his room in reflection upon his course of action. He changed his mind and remained there.

Shortly thereafter, he attended McGready's revival and came away profoundly impressed. He struggled for months to "get religion." In the spring of 1791, he heard William Hodge, a Methodist, preach on the love of God. Stone concluded from this sermon that he could be saved, as he said in his own words:

> I loved Him [Christ]—I adored Him—I praised Him aloud in the silent of the night. . . . I confessed to the Lord my sins and folly in disbelieving His word so long, and in following so long the devices of men. I now saw that a poor sinner was as much authorized to believe in Jesus at first as at last (alluding to the Calvinistic doctrine)—that *now* was the accepted time, and the day of salvation.[6]

Stone became intensely interested in Bible study. He determined to become a preacher and accordingly obtained a license to preach from the Orange Presbytery. He later moved to Cane Ridge, Kentucky. There he was ordained to preach in the Presbyterian Church. However, Stone had not made up his mind to accept all of the Presbyterian doctrines. He had serious doubts about some doctrines in the *Confession of Faith*—the creed of the Presbyterian Church. In fact, at his ordination upon being asked: "Do you receive and adopt the *Confession of Faith*, as containing the system of doctrine as taught in the Bible?" He replied, "I do, as far as I see it consistent with the Word of God."[7]

As he began to preach, Stone made his appeal directly to the Scriptures and his views were considered unorthodox by most of the Presbyterians who were strict Calvinists. He did not preach the Calvinism to which they were accustomed. He exhorted the people from the Scriptures to obey the Lord.

The real division came at a meeting of the Kentucky Synod that condemned the revivalist preaching which was being conducted by Stone and four other Presbyterian preachers at Cane Ridge, Kentucky. These five men separated themselves from the Presbyterian Church to form the "Springfield Presbytery" in September 1803. They sent out letters to all of the churches announcing that they had severed connections with the Presbyterian Church and had abandoned all creeds except the Bible.

---

6 James M. Mathes, *Works of Elder B. W. Stone.* (Cincinnati, OH: Moore, Wilstach, Keys & Co., 1859), 15.
7 Ibid., 17.

This affirmation to stand only upon Bible principles caused them to restudy many of their positions. They hastened to abandon those they concluded to be unscriptural. They came to the conclusion that the forming of a presbytery had no foundation in the Bible. Accordingly, in June 1804, they decided to dissolve this union. They penned a very important document of the Restoration Movement: "The Last Will and Testament of the Springfield Presbytery." Although it contains less than 800 words, it is one of the classical documents coming out of the Restoration Movement.[8]

Years later Stone summarized the importance of this separation from the Presbyterian church as he wrote:

> When we first withdrew, we felt ourselves free from all creeds but the Bible, and since that time by constant application to it, we are led farther from the idea of adopting creeds and confessions as standards, than we were at first; consequently to come under the jurisdiction of that church now is entirely out of the question.[9]

Stone continued to preach in Kentucky. He established churches based upon the New Testament pattern. Stone published a monthly journal entitled *The Christian Messenger*[10] from 1826 through 1845. It is interesting to note that he first met Alexander Campbell at Georgetown, Kentucky in 1824. They became fast friends, but full fellowship was not achieved until 1832. Like those mentioned earlier, Stone arrived at the restoration principle through his own independent study of the Bible. He had no knowledge that many others had arrived at similar conclusions.

4. Thomas Campbell (1763–1854)

It was due to poor health that Thomas Campbell decided to leave his native Ireland in 1807 to journey to North America. He was a minister of the Seceder Presbyterian Church. Upon his arrival in America, he presented himself to the Synod meeting in Philadelphia that year. They assigned him to the Presbytery of Chartiers in Pennsylvania.

The Seceder branch of the Presbyterian Church was very strict in extending fellowship and Campbell's attitude was much too benevolent for them. Campbell sought to be reconciled with the Synod, but his determination to unite different denominations was repulsed.

Many of his friends were in full sympathy with his efforts. Even after the church's doors were closed to him; he continued

---

8 A copy of the document is appended to this study: Appendix E.

9 Charles C. Ware, *Barton Warren Stone, Pathfinder of Christian Union.* (St. Louis, MO: The Bethany Press, 1932), 145.

10 See bibliography for details.

NOTES

to preach in school houses, barns, under the trees and in farm houses. People flocked to hear him plead for unity upon the basis of the scriptural order of things. He set forth a principle that would guide him for the rest of his life: "Speak where the Bible speaks and be silent where the Bible is silent."

In 1808 his family joined him in America. His son, Alexander, united his efforts to those of his father in the restoration plea. On September 8, 1809, Thomas Campbell preached his famous sermon "Declaration and Address," that became another of the great documents supporting Christian unity.[11] Some of the principles stated in this sermon were:

- There is but one church of Christ.
- There ought not be any schisms or divisions.
- Nothing should be taught as articles of faith or terms of communion but what is expressly enjoined in the Word of God.
- The New Testament is the constitution for the worship, discipline, and government of the New Testament Church.
- If the Scripture is silent on a point, no human authority has the right to make laws for the church.
- Those who realize they are lost and are willing to profess faith in Christ and obedience to Him according to His word should be admitted to the church; and,
- Human expedients may be necessary to the fulfillment of a command, but should never be adopted by causing contention or division in the church.[12]

5. Alexander Campbell (1788–1866)

Alexander Campbell arrived in North American in 1808. He was destined to become one of the great exponents of the restoration principle and one of the great leaders of the country. He was recognized as a world renowned scholar. As a young man he read Greek and Latin and spoke French fluently. He committed to memory voluminous amounts of information from literature and history.

Carroll Ellis, late professor of Restoration Literature at David Lipscomb University, gave the following as reasons for Alexander Campbell's becoming the most outstanding person in the Restoration Movement:[13]

---

11 See a summary in Douglas Foster, et. al., *The Encyclopedia of the Stone-Campbell Movement.*(Grand Rapids, MI: William B. Eerdmans Publishing Company, 2004), 263-265.

12 Adapted from Shepherd, 1954: 184-187.

13 From personal class notes in Restoration Preaching, David Lipscomb College, 1955.

- His extensive knowledge of a variety of subjects. I have a book of Campbell's lectures in my library covering the subjects: Social Science, Moral Philosophy, Literature, The Destiny of the Country, Education, Public Schools, Demonology, Soil Conservation, and etc.[14]

- His powerful preaching. He was recognized as an outstanding orator. In June 1850, he preached before both houses of Congress in Washington, D.C. Henry Clay, James Madison, and other notables traveled many miles to hear him preach. Madison said of Campbell, "I regard him as the ablest and most original expounder of Scripture I ever heard."[15]

- His almost unlimited capacity for work. Campbell edited a monthly magazine; taught in a school that he founded at Bethany (now in West Virginia); preached an average of four sermons a week; wrote sixty books; participated in numerous debates; was a successful farmer; and, twice annually, conducted preaching tours in neighboring states. He also corresponded with people all over the world.

- He possessed an aggressive spirit and had the ability to turn this spirit into proper channels. He was very pointed in disagreement but was constructive and would not delve in personalities. He held hotly contested debates with N. L. Rice (Presbyterian); Bishop Purcell (Roman Catholic); and, Robert Owen (Atheist). They all admired him for his gentlemanly conduct.

Upon his arrival in America he entered enthusiastically into the work that his father had begun. They chose a site near their home and constructed a meeting house for worship known as the Brush Run Church. Here, Alexander Campbell preached his first sermon on September 16, 1810.

In 1813, the Brush Run Church became a member of the Redstone Baptist Association. This attachment has been understood by some as meaning that Campbell accepted the Baptist doctrine. To the contrary, neither of the Campbells accepted the Baptist doctrine on baptism nor did they subscribe to the Philadelphia Confession of Faith. In fact, many Baptists heaped abuse upon them.

To the charges made, even in his day, that he was establishing another denomination, Campbell clearly replied:

> I have no idea of adding to the catalogue of new sects. This game
> has been played too long. I labor to see sectarianism abolished,

---

14 A. Campbell, *Popular Lectures and Addresses.* (Nashville, TN: Harbinger Book Club, n.d.).

15 Foster (2004): 123.

NOTES

and all Christians of every name united upon the one foundation on which the apostolic church was founded. To bring Baptist and Paido-Baptist to this is my supreme end. But to connect myself with any people who would require me to sacrifice one item of revealed truth, to subscribe any creed of human device, or to restrain me from publishing my sentiments as discretion and conscience direct, is now, and I hope ever shall be, the farthest from my desired, and the most incompatible with my views.[16]

Writing on the "ancient order of things," Campbell stated:

But *a restoration of the ancient order of things,* is all that is contemplated by the wise disciples of the Lord, as it is agreed that this is all that is wanting to the perfection, happiness, and glory of the Christian community. To contribute to this is our most ardent desire—our daily inquiry and pursuit. Now in attempting this, it must be observed, that it belongs to every individual and to every congregation of individuals to discard from their faith and their practice every thing that is not found written in the New Testament of the Lord and Saviour, and to believe and practice whatever is there enjoined. This done, and every thing is done which ought to be done.[17]

Both *The Christian Baptist* and later *The Millennial Harbinger* that Campbell began publishing in 1830 were opened to other writers and religious topics were thoroughly examined over the course of many years.

6. It is not possible for us to examine the contributions of many others who took up the plea for undenominational Christianity. I have obtained great blessings by reading the biographies, sermons and published journals of many of these leaders, such as: Walter Scott, Moses E. Lard, "Raccoon" John Smith, Benjamin Franklin, Tolbert Fanning, J. W. McGarvey, and David Lipscomb.

None of the leaders of the Restoration Movement considered their efforts a "finished work." It was an on-going process even as it is today. Over the years I have been asked many times, "What do you think about this or that subject?" I have learned to reply, "It doesn't make any difference what *I think*! But *what does God say in His revealed Word on the subject?* In the day of judgment, we will be "judged from the things which were written in the books, according to their [our] deeds" (Rev. 20:12).

---

16 Alexander Campbell, *The Christian Baptist.* 8 Vols. (Nashville, TN: Gospel Advocated Company, 1956), 7: 146.

17 Campbell, *Christian Baptist,* 8:152.

NOTES

Points to Ponder

1. (a. Rice Haggard; b. James O'Kelly; c. Tolbert Fanning) was a great Methodist preacher who desired the unity of believers.

2. (a. The "Five Cardinal Principles"; b. The Sermon on the Law; c. "The Last Will and Testament") was a result of a meeting of those who left the Methodist church in AD 1795.

3. The scattered movements toward the restoration of Christian unity (a. were; b. were not) directed by one group of men.

4. Match the names of these restoration leaders with the event listed below: Alexander Campbell, Thomas Campbell, Barton W. Stone, Rice Haggard, James O'Kelly, Abner Jones, and Elias Smith.

_____ Preached in Virginia and North Carolina.

_____ Urged the "Republican Methodist" to be known only as Christians.

_____ A physician who left the Baptist Church to be a Christian only.

_____ Preached in Vermont with the result of several churches renouncing denominational creeds.

_____ President of Bethany college in Virginia (later it became West Virginia).

_____ Preached two famous restoration sermons: "Declaration and Address" and "The Sermon on the Law."

_____ Debated Presbyterian, Roman Catholic, and atheist opponents.

_____ A successful businessman and farmer in addition to being a preacher and editor.

_____ Edited *The Christian Messenger* for many years.

C. Division in the Restoration Movement Churches

The plea for the restoration of the ancient order of the New Testament spread rapidly across the United States. Thousands renounced human creeds and doctrines to stand upon the Word of God. But about the middle of the nineteenth century a terrible division occurred. This division ultimately brought about the formation of the Christian Church by those who desired to use instruments of music in worship. Certainly other factors were involved as well.

Many Christians opposed the formation of the American Christian Missionary Society in 1849. David Burnett, and others, had held informal meetings in several states to promote the idea of organization of societies on a national level. In 1844, he moved to the Sycamore Street church in Cincinnati. In January of the following year, he called a meeting of representatives of four churches in Cincinnati. They formed the American Christian Bible Society with Burnett serving as president. They formed the Sunday School and Tract Society in 1848. The natural next step was to form a national missionary society. Many Christians were against these societies because no examples of such were found in the New Testament. They argued that the only form of church government authorized in the New Testament is the local autonomous church.

The final rupture came about over the question of instrumental music in worship. The first instruments were introduced in the church at Midway, Kentucky in 1850. Many members of the congregation opposed the introduction of a melodeon into their worship. Isaac Errett of Lexington, Kentucky spearheaded the drive to get the church to accept instrumental music. He accepted it as an *expedient*, never on the basis that the New Testament authorized their use.

Those who opposed their introduction did so on the following grounds: (1) They were not used by the first century Christians although they were freely used in pagan and Jewish worship. (2) God prescribed a pattern of worship. Man does not have the liberty to add to it.[18] (3) God's instruction to "sing" excludes other types of music.

The Christian Church that was formed by those who accept the societies and the use of instruments of music has since divided. Departures from the New Testament always have dreadful consequences. Men and women of good will continue to support the validity of the restoration principles as the only means of achieving Christian unity. They also know that restoration is always an on-going process. We must continue to examine all issues in the light of the authority of Christ and His apostles revealed to us in the New Testament.

18 1 Corinthians 4:6; Mark 7:7; Revelation 22:18.

Now Let's Review

(Are the statements listed below true or false? Answer in the space provided. Then review Part IV to see how well you answered each statement.)

_____ 1. The restoration movement was an attempt by a group of men working together in various parts of the United States to return to undenominational Christianity.

_____ 2. The restoration leaders felt that existing denominations should be reformed.

_____ 3. James O'Kelly led in one of the earliest known attempts at restoration.

_____ 4. Rice Haggard was insistent that the name "Methodist" be retained.

_____ 5. Elias Smith, a Baptist preacher, urged the restoration of New Testament teaching in Vermont.

_____ 6. Barton W. Stone subscribed without reservation to the Presbyterian *Confession of Faith*.

_____ 7. Thomas Campbell urged his son to remain in the Presbyterian fellowship.

_____ 8. Alexander Campbell arrived in the United States several years after the beginning of the Restoration Movement.

_____ 9. The Campbells sought to begin a new denomination.

_____ 10. David Burnett led in establishing the missionary societies.

_____ 11. Instrumental music in worship brought about a division in the church at Midway, Kentucky.

_____ 12. Early supporters of the use of musical instruments in worship did so on the grounds of "expediency" not Scripture.

Part V

Rediscovering the Restoration Plea[1]

My *Survey of Church History* has been out of print for many years. It became clear to me that while doing the revision that it would be necessary to address the current literature being written by some in our fellowship who either deny the validity of the Restoration Plea outright or would modify it in some way. To this end, I have read most of the books and articles published since 1980 by those who claim membership in churches of Christ, but no longer hold to strict Restoration principles. Some churches in our fellowship have discontinued the use of "church of Christ" to define who they are.[2] This is not, in and of itself, a departure from the Restoration Plea since the New Testament uses many names to describe the church. However, some of them have added instrumental music in their worship and women in public worship leadership roles. Neither of these reflect the teaching of the New Testament and are departures from the Restoration Plea.

I firmly believe in the validity of the Restoration Plea. It should be emphasized that this does not mean a return to the teachings of Alexander Campbell, Barton W. Stone or a host of eighteenth and nineteenth century Christians who also realized the need for Rediscovering the Restoration Plea. While admiring their courage and study that led them to seek unity on the principles of the Bible alone; rediscovering the restoration plea means simply returning to the Word of God as the sole authority and the recognition that Jesus is Lord of our lives.

I have no intention of entering into a lengthy discussion of the many books and articles of those insisting on "change" within our fellowship. I merely wish to reflect on what seems to me to be assumptions that issue from their writing.[3]

---

1 I am indebted to my colleague, Jim Bury for this title. He used it in an article in Church and Family, Summer 2002, 22–23, published by Harding University, Searcy, AR.

2 Let it be clearly understood that "church of Christ" is not an exclusive name for God's people in the Bible. See "Designations in the New Testament for the Church," p. 7.

3 I am not judging the motives of these writers. I am sure they are sincere in their own minds. I simply do not agree with them based on my own Bible study.

NOTES

A. Obstacles to Rediscovering the Restoration Plea
1. Intellectual Arrogance

The first obstacle seems to be an intellectual arrogance which assumes that the change agents know the hearts and minds of the "conservative" brethren throughout our fellowship. It seems that they are painting a broad picture sometimes accusing Christians in the smaller congregations of being "behind the times," "unspiritual," and "unloving." As they are painting this picture which indicts our brotherhood, I would ask them: Do you know the brotherhood well enough to do this? Have you been in hundreds of small congregations throughout the United States and the world?

That these smaller congregations should be characterized in this way has not been my impression at all. I grew up in a small congregation in western Oklahoma. I have returned there several times to preach in the last few years. They love the Lord and each other. They do many works of benevolence and evangelism. Just because they worship almost the same way each Lord's Day does not mean they are lacking in spirituality. I am glad that each congregation is autonomous. This keeps them from being overly influenced by the "change agents" amongst us.

2. Instruments of Music in Worship

Second, it seems clear to me that they have abandoned the Restoration Plea to "Speak where the Bible Speaks, and be Silent where the Bible is Silent," on the issue of instruments of music in worship. There is absolutely no justification in the Bible for the use of instruments of music in Christian worship. This fact is attested to by scholars of all religious persuasions.[4]

What we are hearing today is: "Instrumental music is not a salvation issue." In recent years I have heard it many times including from an elder in the church and a professor at a Christian university. I asked both of them, "How do you know?" Neither could give an answer to that question. As I see the clarity of God's demands for Israelite worship to be according to His commands, I am convinced that Christian worship is to be as the Lord through His apostles gave it to us in the apostolic churches and Scripture.

3. "Believers" and the Community Church Movement

Third, some are abandoning the Restoration Plea to follow the community church model. Today, I am hearing those who speak of "believers" instead of "Christians." The term "believer"

4 See an old, but reliable work: M. C. Kurfees, *Instrumental Music in the Worship.* (Nashville, TN: Gospel Advocate Co., 1950).

is being used to describe both the immersed and un-immersed believers. It is being used as a term offering fellowship to those of various denominations or to those of "undenominational" affiliation. Church leaders must wake up to the fact that many of our young people are embracing the community church model. The fellowship of these community churches is, of necessity, based on the lowest common denominator doctrinally. One must confess faith in Jesus Christ, therefore be a "believer." Beyond that, a good ethical life is demanded. But doctrine has been relegated to a secondary place. Strict adherence to the doctrine of Christ in the New Testament would be "divisive" in the eyes of many in these churches. Thus, they settle on fellowship with anyone who is a "Believer."

Certainly we should be kind and loving toward all people regardless of their religious affiliation. We must always speak "the truth in love, we are to grow up in all aspects into Him who is the head, even Christ" (Eph. 4:15). We must desire to "sanctify Christ as Lord in your hearts, always being ready to make a defense to everyone who asks you to give an account for the hope that is in you, yet with gentleness and reverence" (1 Pet. 3:15). But we must be true to our biblical convictions and not compromise them.

4. Biblical Illiteracy

Fourth, a major obstacle to Rediscovering the Restoration Plea is biblical illiteracy. As Christians we know that the Bible is our spiritual food for the soul. Yet many are letting the "worry of the world and the deceitfulness of wealth choke the word, and it become[s] unfruitful" (Matt. 13:22). Do you, as a Christian, have a systematic Bible study plan? Have you ever read the Bible through in a year? Does your congregation have a good Bible study program for all ages? Do you bring your Bible to worship and classes so that you can follow the lessons being taught? I remember my good friend, the late Richard Rogers, saying in worship, "Thank God for the rustling of the leaves." He was referring to Christians turning to the text cited to read it as he was preaching. Because of biblical illiteracy, "doctrine" has become a word seldom heard among Christians today. In fact, some would insist that we not "indoctrinate" young people! The apostle Paul urged the young preachers Titus and Timothy and elders in the church to maintain sound [i.e. healthy] doctrine.

To Timothy he said:

> In pointing out these things to the brethren, you will be a good servant of Christ Jesus, *constantly nourished on the words of the faith and of the sound doctrine* which you have been following (1 Tim. 4:6, Emphasis mine, ds).

NOTES

If anyone advocates a different doctrine and does not agree with sound words, those of our Lord Jesus Christ, and with the doctrine conforming to godliness, he is conceited and understands nothing; but he has a morbid interest in controversial questions and disputes about words, out of which arise envy, strife, abusive language, evil suspicions, and constant friction between men of depraved mind and deprived of the truth, who suppose that godliness is a means of gain (1 Tim. 6:3–5).

I solemnly charge you in the presence of God and of Christ Jesus, who is to judge the living and the dead, and by His appearing and His kingdom: *preach the word*; be ready in season and out of season; reprove, rebuke, exhort, with great patience and instruction. For the time will come when *they will not endure sound doctrine*; but wanting to have their ears tickled, *they will accumulate for themselves teachers in accordance to their own desires, and will turn away their ears from the truth and will turn aside to myths* (2 Tim. 4:1–4, Emphasis mine, ds).

Of the elders he said:

For the overseer must be above reproach as God's steward, not self-willed, not quick-tempered, not addicted to wine, not pugnacious, not fond of sordid gain, but hospitable, loving what is good, sensible, just, devout, self-controlled, *holding fast the faithful word* which is in accordance with the teaching, so that he will be able *both to exhort in sound doctrine and to refute those who contradict* (Titus 1:7–9, Emphasis mine, ds).

To Titus he wrote: "But as for you, speak the things which are fitting for sound doctrine" (Titus 2:1).

To the elders (shepherds) at Ephesus he declared:

And now, behold, I know that all of you, among whom I went about preaching the kingdom, will no longer see my face. Therefore, I testify to you this day that I am innocent of the blood of all men. *For I did not shrink from declaring to you the whole purpose of God.* Be on guard for yourselves and for all the flock, among which the Holy Spirit has made you overseers, to shepherd the church of God which He purchased with His own blood. I know that after my departure savage wolves will come in among you, not sparing the flock; and from among your own selves men will arise, speaking perverse things, to draw away the disciples after them. Therefore be on the alert, remembering that night and day for a period of three years I did not cease to admonish each one with tears. And now *I commend you to God and to the word of His grace, which is able to build you up and to give you the inheritance among all those who are sanctified* (Acts 20:25–32, Emphasis mine, ds).

As we read all of these solemn encouragements and warnings, can we fail to be concerned about sound doctrine? Must we leave it to a few to do our Bible study? Of course not! It is the duty of every Christian to "present yourself approved to God as a workman who does not need to be ashamed, *accurately handling the word of truth*" (2 Tim. 3:15, Emphasis mine, ds).

5. Meeting "Felt" Needs in Worship

Fifth, the desire of congregations to emphasize meeting "felt" needs in worship can hinder Rediscovering the Restoration Principle. Too frequently one hears, "I did not get anything out of worship today!" My reply to those who say this is, "What did you put into worship today?" In Christian worship, the only spectator is God! All Christians are participants in mutual edification and praise to Him!

In speaking of the worship experience, Harris and Shelly have well said:

> Is the term "worship experience" misleading in itself? Some think so and object to it because it suggests that worship is important by reason of the feelings it can produce in participants. Whether the term itself is objectionable, we leave to the taste of each reader; the notion of reducing worship to warm and pleasing feelings called forth in participants is simply wrong-headed. Though worship frequently generates good experiences and leaves one with pleasant feelings, neither the experience nor the attendant feeling is correctly termed worship. That many are unable to make this distinction is evidenced by the fact that they are quick to judge the entertainment value of a church service while remaining unfamiliar with the reality to which it can open us.[5]

They add:

> To create settings that deliberately manipulate emotions and tantalize participants is cheap theater rather than worship. Or, if one insists on calling it worship, it is self-worship rather than the worship of God. True worship does not call attention to itself; it serves instead as a means for focusing attention on God.[6]

Points to Ponder

1. What is the cause of "intellectual arrogance"?
2. Discuss the issue of instrumental music and "salvation issues."
3. Why is it not proper to designate "believers" as also being "Christians?"
4. What are dangers of biblical illiteracy?
5. Discuss why "felt needs" may or may not be met in a worship service.

---

5 Randall J. Harris & Rubel Shelly, *The Second Incarnation: Empowering the Church for the 21st Century.* (West Monroe, LA: Howard Publishing Co., 1992), 120.
6 Ibid., 121.

NOTES

B. Characteristics Needed in Rediscovering the Restoration Plea
  1. Love of Truth

First, a characteristic for Rediscovering the Restoration Plea is an absolute commitment to and a love of truth. When our Lord was being tried at the tribunal of Pilate, he asked Jesus: "What is truth?" (John 18:38). Jesus had already given His disciples the answer to this question in His final prayer to the Father:

> I have given them *Your word;* and the world has hated them, because they are not of the world, even as I am not of the world. I do not ask You to take them out of the world, but to keep them from the evil one. They are not of the world, even as I am not of the world. *Sanctify them in the truth; Your word is truth* (John 17:14–17, emphasis mine, ds).

In 1984, the noted apologist, Francis A Schaffer, wrote *The Great Evangelical Disaster*. He defined it by saying:

> Here is the great evangelical disaster—the failure of the evangelical world to stand for truth as truth. There is only one word for this— namely *accommodation:* the evangelical church has accommodated to the world spirit of the age. First, there has been accommodation on Scripture, so that many who call themselves evangelicals hold a weakened view of the Bible and no longer affirm the truth of all the Bible teaches—truth not only in religious matters but in the areas of science and history and morality.[7]

In 1988, Carl F. H. Henry, the founding editor of *Christianity Today* sounded a solemn warning: "Our generation is lost to the truth of God, to the reality of divine revelation, to the content of God's will, to the power of his redemption, and to the authority of His Word."[8]

A recent lecturer at a Christian university spoke on the postmodern denial of truth. He said, "Religion is thought of as the product of human thinking and not as the response of men to the God who is really there.... The new emphasis in religion is therefore not on reason and understanding, but upon intuition and feeling. In the realm of the non-rational, there can be *no categories* of truth or non-truth and no moral categories of right and wrong."[9]

A Christian in any century will be fully committed to these facts: The Bible is the inspired word of God; The Bible is true

---

7 Francis A. Schaffer, *The Great Evangelical Disaster.* (Westchester, IL: Crossway Books, 1984), 37.
8 Carl F. H. Henry, *The Twilight of a Great Civilization: The Drift toward Neo-Paganism.* (Westchester, IL: Crossway Books, 1988), 15.
9 Jim Baird, Lectures delivered at Harding University, "Postmodernism: A Changing World-View,"10.

and complete in every sense; and, The New Testament is the pattern for the church and for Christian living.

2. A Desire for Unity of All Believers

A second characteristic will be the desire for unity of all Christians in the one body—the church. This unity must be based on the teachings of the New Testament and on the Lord Jesus Christ. As Jim Bury said, "We must stress the central teachings of Christianity rather than simply highlighting our differences with others. . . . We cannot let disagreements define us."[10] He is not suggesting that we downplay how the church worships or the way it is structured, but the church's defining traits must be centered around Jesus.[11]

3. A Humble Spirit

Christians in their zeal to promote New Testament Christianity have sometimes appeared to be prideful and mean spirited. We must all realize that we are disciples (i.e., learners) and that we should be ready to learn from anyone who speaks to us. Let us have the humility and spirit of the Bereans who, "received the word with great eagerness, examining the Scriptures *daily* to see whether these things were so" (Acts 17:11, emphasis mine).

Points to Ponder

1. Discuss how one may know (be certain) of truth.
2. What is the only basis for unity of all believers?
3. What is the biblical mandate for humility?

Conclusion

Rediscovering the Restoration Plea is an ongoing process for every Christian. We must be dedicated to following Christ and His teachings. We must always examine what we do and why we do it in the light of God's Word. We must have the courage to change when we discover that we have been wrong on any biblical issue. We must rekindle our evangelistic zeal to reach sinners. We must teach our children and grandchildren the Bible with passion. We must guard against false teachers within and without the church. We must never compromise our conscience.

May our God and Father and the Lord Jesus Christ helps us in the continuing Rediscovering of the Restoration Plea.

---

10 Bury, 23.
11 Ibid.

NOTES

Now Let's Review

(Answer these true-false statements without looking at the material that you have studied. Then turn back and review the material to see how many you answered correctly).

_____ 1. Challenges have arisen against the Restoration Plea from within the fellowship of churches of Christ.

_____ 2. It is a sin to call the church anything but "church of Christ."

_____ 3. Intellectual arrogance implies that the person has broad, comprehensive knowledge with which to judge.

_____ 4. Instrumental music is not a salvation issue.

_____ 5. "Believers," in the biblical sense, are those who also obey the will of God.

_____ 6. Doctrine is no longer important in modern times.

_____ 7. Biblical illiteracy is a grave problem in the church today.

_____ 8. It is the duty of elders to guard the church against false doctrine and practice.

_____ 9. It is important that "felt needs" be met every time one worships.

_____ 10. Two noted theologians assert that there is not a "love of truth" today.

_____ 11. A Bible professor recently said that the new emphasis in religion is upon "intuition and feeling."

_____ 12. Unity of all Christians in the one body (church) is a worthy goal.

_____ 13. Paul commended the Bereans because they received his word and examined the Scriptures to see whether his words were so.

Appendix A

A Study of the Greek Word ἐκκλησία from Which We Derive "Church"

I. It refers to an "assembly" of any kind.

A. Christian (see below)

B. Pagan

So then, some were shouting one thing and some another, for the *assembly* was in confusion, and the majority did not know for what cause they had come together (Acts 19:32).[1]

But if you want anything beyond this, it shall be settled in the lawful *assembly*. For indeed we are in danger of being accused of a riot in connection with today's affair, since there is no real cause for it; and in this connection we shall be unable to account for this disorderly gathering. And after saying this he dismissed the *assembly* (Acts 19:39–42).

C. Jewish

This is the Moses who said to the sons of Israel, "God shall raise up for you a prophet like me from your brethren." This is the one who was in the *congregation* in the wilderness together with the angel who was speaking to him on Mount Sinai, and who was with our fathers; and he received living oracles to pass on to you (Acts 7:37–38).

I will proclaim Thy name to My brethren, In the midst of the *congregation* I will sing Thy praise (Heb. 2:12).

II. The *Ekklesia* of Christ—the Church

A. An Actual Assembly of Christians

So Peter was kept in the prison, but prayer for him was being made fervently by the *church* to God (Acts 12:5).

And when they had arrived and gathered the *church* together, they began to report all things that God had done with them and how He had opened a door of faith to the Gentiles (Acts 14:27).

Therefore, being sent on their way by the *church,* they were passing through both Phoenicia and Samaria, describing in detail the conversion of the Gentiles, and were bringing great joy to all the brethren (Acts 15:3).

---

1 I have highlighted words for emphasis in the various Bible passages quoted.

Acts 18:22 And when he had landed at Caesarea, he went up and greeted the *church,* and went down to Antioch (Acts 18:22).[2]

B. Christians Who Assemble (Whether Actually Assembled or Not)
1. In a local sense:

And great fear came upon the whole *church,* and upon all who heard of these things (Acts 5:11).

And Saul was in hearty agreement with putting him to death. And on that day a great persecution arose against the *church* in Jerusalem; and they were all scattered throughout the regions of Judea and Samaria, except the apostles (Acts 8:1).

But Saul began ravaging the *church*, entering house after house; and dragging off men and women, he would put them in prison (Acts 8:3).

I commend to you our sister Phoebe, who is a servant of the *church* which is at Cenchrea (Rom. 16:1).

To the *church* of God which is at Corinth, to those who have been sanctified in Christ Jesus, saints by calling, with all who in every place call upon the name of our Lord Jesus Christ, their Lord and ours (1 Cor. 1:2).

And all the brethren who are with me, to the *churches* of Galatia (Gal. 1:2).

Paul and Silvanus and Timothy to the *church* of the Thessalonians in God the Father and the Lord Jesus Christ: Grace to you and peace (1 Thess. 1:1).[3]

2. In the *universal* sense of all believers that form the one body in Christ:

And I also say to you that you are Peter, and upon this rock I will build My *church*; and the gates of Hades shall not overpower it (Matt. 16:18).

So the *church* throughout all Judea and Galilee and Samaria enjoyed peace, being built up; and, going on in the fear of the Lord and in the comfort of the Holy Spirit, it continued to increase (Acts 9:31).

---

2 See also 1 Corinthians 14:4, 5, 12, 19, 28, 34, 34; 2 Corinthians 11:18.
3 This is a very frequent use of ἐκκλησία. See also these examples that are not exhaustive: Acts 11:22; 112:1; 13:1; 14:23; 15:4, 22, 41; 16:5; Romans 16:4-5, 16, 22; 1 Corinthians 4:17; 6:4; 11:16, 22; Philippians 4:15; Colossians 4:15–16; 1 Timothy 3:5; Philemon 2; James 5:14; Revelation 1:4–5, 11, 20; 2:1, 7, 8, 11.

And God has appointed in the *church,* first apostles, second prophets, third teachers, then miracles, then gifts of healings, helps, administrations, various kinds of tongues (1 Cor. 12:28).

And He put all things in subjection under His feet, and gave Him as head over all things to the *church*, which is His body, the fulness of Him who fills all in all (Eph. 1:22–23).

I am writing these things to you, hoping to come to you before long; but in case I am delayed, I write so that you may know how one ought to conduct himself in the household of God, which is the *church* of the living God, the pillar and support of the truth (1 Tim. 3:14–15).[4]

---

4 See other examples of this use: Matthew 18:18; Galatians 1:13; Ephesians 3:10, 21; 5:23–32; Philippians 3:6; Hebrews 12:23.

Appendix B

Early Ecumenical (General) Councils

The first seven Roman Catholic Councils are listed with some of the doctrines discussed or adopted by them:[1]

1. The Council of Nicaea (AD 325).
   It was called by Emperor Constantine I, who presided over the sessions. He hoped the council would resolve the problem of the heresy promoted by Arius of Alexandria who taught that Jesus Christ is not divine but a created being. The council condemned Arius who was exiled. It also discussed the proper method for consecrating bishops, the rights of metropolitans, the time of Easter and condemned clerics lending money at interest. It issued the Nicene Creed that was later refined at the Council of Constantinople.[2]

2. The Council of Constantinople (AD 381).
   It was called by the Emperor Theodosius. It confirmed the Nicene Creed and discussed the doctrine of the equality of the Holy Spirit with the Father and the Son. It also gave the bishop of Constantinople precedence of honor over all other bishops except the bishop of Rome.

3. The Council of Ephesus (AD 431).
   It was called to discuss the heresies of Nestorius. It debated the two natures of Christ (physical and spiritual). Mary was declared the "Mother of God."

4. The Council of Chalcedon (AD 451).
   It was attended by about 520 bishops or their representatives. It reconfirmed the Nicene Creed and rejected the Monophysite doctrine that Christ had only one nature.

5. The Second Council of Constantinople (AD 553).
   The council issued fourteen anathemas including one against the Nestorian doctrine. The Roman Pope refused to accept the validity of the council at first. But later ratified its proceedings.

6. The Third Council of Constantinople (AD 680).
   It condemned the doctrines of Monothelitism who sought to enforce the unity of the one person of Christ by talking of one will *(thelema)* and one operation *(energeia)* from the two natures.

7. The Second Council of Nicea (AD 787).
   It asserted that icons (images) deserved reverence and veneration.

---

1 For more information on these general councils consult: *Merriam-Webster's Encyclopedia of World Religions.* Wendy Doniger, Consulting Editor. Springfield, MA: Merriam-Webster, Incorporated, 1999.

2 See a translation of the Nicene Creed that is accepted by Roman Catholics, Eastern Orthodox, Anglican, and some major Protestant churches in: *Merriam-Wesbster's Encyclopedia of World Religions:* 810.

Appendix C

Who Shall Save Me?

When Saul of Tarsus realized that he was hopelessly and helplessly lost under a law of works which he could not keep to perfection and which was impotent to save him from his sins, he cried out in grief and anxiety, "O wretched man that I am, who shall save me from the body of this death?" The answer he found brought a joy and peace to his soul which he had never before known, and which he was to carry to his death years later, "Jesus Christ our Lord." The unfortunate Catholic who has a sensitive conscience finds himself in the same condition as did Saul, and he cries out as did Saul, "Who shall save me?" but the answers he receives from his priestly advisers bring him neither peace nor assurance. Rather they leave him to live out his life in doubt and anxiety, and to die in complete uncertainty. Probably no aspect of the Catholic doctrine is more fiendish than that aspect which continually threatens the Catholics with hell-fire, while always holding just beyond their grasp the assurance of salvation.

A faithful Catholic goes to the priest to confess his sins in order to have remission of these sins. He has been taught that he must confess in detail every sin of thought or action, and that if he voluntarily fails to confess any sin, he is committing a mortal sin, his confession is not valid, and he will not have the remission of the sins he did confess. But even the confessor who is reasonably certain he has confessed all his sins, cannot rest in peace even when he hears the priest repeat the magic formula *ego te absolvo,* "I absolve you," for with this the priest gives him remission only for the guilt of sin, and not the temporal punishment of sin which one must suffer either in this life, or in purgatory.

According to this doctrine, a person might have the remission of all his sins when he dies, and yet go to purgatory to suffer no one knows how long for these very sins which have been remitted. So in order to have remission from the penalty of sins, one must do penance, or good works. The system is such, however, that no ordinary person need ever hope to do enough good works to counter-balance the evil he does. Only the saints who have lived a life of asceticism and poverty have been able to accumulate more merits than demerits, and that which they have left over has been put in the great church-treasury to be put at the disposal of the less pious folks in the form of indulgences.

Thus by doing certain pious acts prescribed by the church and usually accompanied by a nominal outlay of money, a person can avail himself of the church's great storehouse of merits, and thus escape also the suffering in purgatory—this, of course, in theory. In practice, however, the Catholic finds no more consolation in the doctrine of indulgences than he does in any other of the church's ambiguous teachings. He never knows just how much demerit is attached to any given sin, and does not know if he will need a hundred years' indulgences to cover it, or ten thousand. And of course he cannot pile up indulgences to serve for future sins, so he is in eternal search for these indulgences, hoping against hope, that he may acquire enough to at least shorten considerably his stay in the flames of purgatory.

But this is not the only deceitful thing about indulgences. The Catholic apologists vehemently denounce non-Catholics for misrepresenting them, and particularly so with regard to indulgences. But the truth about the matter is that the priests themselves mislead their own people. How then can they expect the non-Catholics to understand their doctrines? An ordinary Catholic in Rome who visits a certain church in order to obtain a ten-year indulgence thinks he is diminishing by ten years his stay in purgatory, but it is not at all true. What the priests have failed to tell him is that the ten years refer not to the amount of time cut off the purgatory sentence, but rather to the amount of merit obtained, i.e., the man visiting the church obtained with that one act as much merit as a saint obtained by doing good works for ten years. So the poor fellow doesn't know what he has earned; he doesn't know how or why he has earned it, nor how much good it will do him to have earned it.

There is even the possibility of obtaining a plenary, or full indulgence. Particularly in Rome, the possibilities are almost unlimited, so he who does not obtain a full indulgence is either a non-believer, or lazy. However, there is one catch that the "faithful" do not know about. A person must be in such an elevated state spiritually in order to obtain this indulgence that it is almost impossible for an ordinary person to succeed. In fact in AD 1900 when the "Holy Door"[1] was opened, Pope Leo XIII is reported to have said that in his judgment only one old lady of all the thousands of thousands who went through it really obtained the indulgence.

What is the church's scope in all this? The same as her scope in everything she does—to keep her people totally and blindly dependent upon her, and to drain them of every penny possible. Indulgences are a Middle Age invention of the priests, and until forced by the Reformation Movement to discontinue the practice, the priests sold the indulgences at fixed prices. Priests today would have all non-Catholics believe that the "pay and pray" practices in the church have all been eliminated, and though the Council of Trent, condemned many of the abuses connected with indulgence, selling, and etc., the practice in Catholic countries today is not much different than in the Middle Ages. Take for example the mass said for the dead. You can stop anyone on the streets

---

1 The "Holy Door" is one of the large entrances into Saint Peter's Basilica that is opened only once every fifty years for the "faithful" to enter into the edifice.

of Rome and they can tell you the minimum price for that mass in their parish, usually about one dollar.[2] So a rich person can have a thousand masses said for his dead loved one, and thus get him out of purgatory, while the poor person will just have to stand his chances with the devil. Not only so, but the indulgences that are no longer sold are usually connected with some particular place such as Rome, Lourdes, Fatima, etc., so that a rich person who is able to travel can go there and get his "free" indulgence, while spending his money instead for Catholic hotels, Catholic souvenirs, Catholic liquor, etc.

So those who have unconcernedly and blindly accepted every fiendish doctrine that greedy, ambitious and warped minds could invent have found an easy convenient way to be defrauded of their money, and worse still, to be deprived of that unpurchasable gift of eternal life that is to be had only through humble obedience to and reliance on Christ.

---

2 Keith Robinson wrote this in the 1960s, so that price is likely much more today.

Appendix D

Origins of Denominations[1]

Denomination	Place	Date	Founder
Adventism	Massachusetts	1831	William Miller
American Baptist	Providence, RI	1639	Roger Williams
Apostolic Faith Mission	United States	1900	Group
Assembly of God	Hot Springs, AR	1914	Group
Baptist Church	London, England	1607	John Smyth
Brethren (Dunkards)	Scwarzenau, Germany	1708	Hochmann & Mack
Brethren in Christ	United States	1820	Group
Catholic Apostolic Church	England	1830	Group
Christian Church	Midway, KY	1859	Group
Christadelphians	United States	1844	John Thomas, M.D.
Christian Science	Boston, MA	1879	Mary Baker Eddy
Church of England	England	1535	Henry VIII
Church of God	Monroe County, TN	1886	Group
Church of God[2]	United States	1880	D. S. Warner
Church of God (Holiness)	Atlanta, GA	1914	K. H. Burrus
Church of the Living God	Wrightsville, AR	1889	William Christian
Congregational Church	Massachusetts	1684	Group
Cumberland Presbyterian	Dickson County, TN	1810	Group
Dutch Reformed Church	Holland	1560	Group
Evangelical Church	Pennsylvania	1803	Jacob Albright
Evangelical and Reformed	Cleveland, OH	1934	Group
Foursquare Gospel	Los Angeles, CA	1917	Aimee McPherson
Freewill Baptist	New Durham, NC	1780	Benjamin Randall
Full Gospel Church	Goldsboro, NC	1935	R. H. Askew
Greek Orthodox	Church Greece	1053	Group
Holiness Church	Chicago, IL	1907	Howard Hoople
House of David	Michigan	1903	Group
Independent Holiness	Van Alstyne, TX	1900	C. B. Jernigan
Jehovah's Witnesses	Pennsylvania	1874	Charles T. Russell
Lutheran Church	Augsburg, Germany	1530	Martin Luther
Mennonite Church	Zurich, Switzerland	1525	Group
Methodist Church	London, England	1729	John Wesley
Methodist Episcopal	Baltimore, MD	1874	Group
Mormon Church	Seneca, NY	1830	Joseph Smith
Mormons (Reorganized)	Wisconsin	1852	Joseph Smith II

---

1 The tabulation was prepared by Waymond D. Miller and is used with his permission.

2 Headquarters at Anderson, Indiana.

Moravian Church	Kunwald, Bohemia	1457	Group
Nazarene Church	Los Angeles, CA	1895	P. F. Bresee
New Apostolic Church	Anderson, SC	1862	Pruess
Pentecostal Holiness	Anderson, SC	1898	Group
Pilgrim Holiness Church	Cincinnati, OH	1897	Group
Plymoth Brethren	Dublin, Ireland	1829	Group
Presbyterian Church	Geneva, Switzerland	1535	John Calvin
Primitive Baptist	North Carolina	1765	Group
Quakers	England	1650	George Fox
Roman Catholic	Rome, Italy	606	Boniface III[3]
Salvation Army	London, England	1865	William Booth
Seventh-Day Adventist	Massachusetts	1846	Ellen G. White
Unitarians	Poland	16th C.	C. Faustus, Socinus
Universalist Church	New Jersey	1770	John Murry

---

3 The first recognized Roman Catholic Pope.

Appendix E

Last Will and Testament of the Springfield Presbytery

For where a testament is, there must of necessity be the death of the testator; for a testament is of force after men are dead, otherwise it is of no strength at all, while the testator liveth. Thou fool that which thou soweth is not quickened except it die. Verily, verily I say unto you, except a corn of wheat fall into the ground, and die, it abideth along; but if it die, it bringeth forth more fruit. Whose voice then shook the earth; but now he hath promised, saying, yet once more I shake not the earth only, but also heaven. And this word, yet once more, signifies the removing of those things that shaken as of thing that are made, that those things which cannot be shaken may remain—Scripture!

Last Will and Testament, &c.

The Presbytery of Springfield, sitting at Cane Ridge, in the county of Bourbon, being, through a gracious Providence, in more than ordinary bodily health and growing in strength and size daily; and in perfect soundness and composure of mind; but knowing that it is appointed for all delegated bodies once to die: and considering that the life of every such body is very uncertain, do make, and ordain this our last Will and Testament, in manner and form following, viz?

Imprimis. We *will*, that this body die, be dissolved, and sink into union with the Body of Christ at large; for there is but one body, and one Spirit, even as we were called in one hope of our calling.

Item. We *will*, that our name of distinction, with its *Reverend* title, be forgotten, that there be but one Lord over God's heritage, and his name one.

Item. We *will*, that our power of making laws for the government of the church, and executing them by delegated authority, forever cease; that the people may have free course to the Bible, and adopt *the law of the spirit of life in Christ Jesus.*

Item. We *will*, that candidates for the Gospel ministry henceforth study the Holy Scriptures with fervent prayer, and obtain license from God to preach the simple gospel, *with the Holy Ghost sent down from heaven*, without any mixture of philosophy, vain deceit, traditions of men, or the rudiments of the world. And let none henceforth *take this honor to himself, but he that is called of God, as was Aaron.*

Item. We *will*, that the church of Christ resume her native right of internal government—try her candidates for the ministry, as to their soundness in the faith, acquaintance with experimental religion, gravity and aptness to teach; and admit no other proof of their authority but Christ speaking in them. We will, that the church send forth laborers into his harvest; and that she resume her primitive right of trying those *who say they are apostles, and are not.*

Item. We *will,* that the people henceforth take the Bible as the only sure guide to heaven; and as many are offended with other books, which stand in competition with it, may cast them into the fire if they choose; for it is better to enter into life having one book, than having many to be cast into hell.

Item. We *will,* that our weak brethren, who may have been wishing to make the Presbytery of Springfield their king, and wot not what is now become of it, betake themselves to the Rock of Ages, and follow Jesus for the future.

Item. We *will,* that the Synod of Kentucky examine every member, who may be *suspected* of having departed from the Confession of Faith, and suspend every such heretic immediately; in order that the oppressed may go free, and taste the sweets of gospel liberty.

Item. We *will,* that Ja........ ...., the author of two letters lately published in Lexicon, Kentucky, be encouraged in his zeal to destroy *partyism.* We will, moreover, that our past conduct be examined into by all who may have correct information; but let foreigners beware of speaking evil of things which they know not.

Item. Finally we *will,* that all our *sister bodies* read their Bibles carefully, that they may see their fate there determined, and prepare for death before it is too late

SPRINGFIELD PRESBYTERY,
June 28th, 1804 L.S.

ROBERT MARSHALL,
JOHN DUNLAVY,
RICHARD M'NEMAR, WITNESSES
B. W. STONE,
JOHN THOMPSON,
DAVID PURVIANCE,

THE WITNESSES' ADDRESS

We, the above named witnesses of the Last Will and Testament of the Springfield Presbytery, knowing that there will be many conjectures respecting the causes which have occasioned the dissolution of that body, think proper to testify, that from its first existence it was knit together in love, lived in peace and concord, and died a voluntary and happy death.

Their reasons for dissolving that body were the following: With deep concern they viewed the divisions, and party spirit among professing Christians, principally owing to the adoption of human creeds and forms of Government. While they were united under the name of the Presbytery, they endeavored to cultivate a spirit of love and unity to suppress the idea that they themselves were a party separate from others. This difficulty increased in proportion to their success in the ministry. Jealousies were excited in the minds of other denominations; and a temptation was laid before those who were connected with the various parties, to view them in the same light. At their last meeting they understood to prepare for the press a piece entitled Observation on Church Government, in which the world will see the beautiful simplicity of Christian church government, stript of human inventions and lordly traditions. As they proceeded in the investigation of that subject, they soon found that there was neither precept nor example in the New Testament for such confederacies as modern Church Sessions, Presbyteries, Synods, General Assemblies, &c. Hence they concluded, that while they continued in the connection in which they then stood, they were off the foundation of the apostles and prophets, of which Christ himself is the chief corner stone. However just, therefore, their views of church government might have been, they would have gone under the name of sanction of a self-constituted body. Therefore, from a principle of love to Christians of every name, the precious cause of Jesus, and dying sinners who are kept form the Lord by the existence of sects and parties in the church, they have cheerfully consented to retire from the din and fury of conflicting parties—sink out of the view of fleshly minds, and die the death. They believe their death will be of great pain to the world. But though death, as above, and stript of their mortal frame, which only served to keep them near the confines of Egyptian bondage, they yet live and speak into the land of gospel liberty; they blow the trumpet of jubilee, and willing devote themselves to the help of the Lord against the mighty. They will aid the brethern, by their counsel, when required; assist in ordaining elders, or pastors—seek the divine blessing—unite with all Christians, commune together, and strengthen each others' hands in the work of the Lord.

We design, by the grace of God, to continue in the exercise of those functions, which belong to us as ministers of the gospel, confidently trusting the Lord, that he will be with us. We candidly acknowledge, that in some things we may err, through human infirmities; but he will correct our wanderings, and preserve his Church. Let all Christians join with us, in crying to God day and night, to remove the obstacles which stand in the way of his work, and give him to rest till he make Jerusalem a praise in the earth. We heartily unite with our Christian brethren in ever name, in the glorious work he is carrying on in our Western country, which we hope will terminate in the universal spread of the gospel, and the unity of the church.

Bibliography

DICTIONARIES AND LEXICONS

William F. Arndt and F. Wilbur Gingrich, Editors and Translators, *A Greek-English Lexicon of the New Testament and Other Early Christian Literature.* (Chicago, IL: University of Chicago Press, 1979).

G. Abbot-Smith, *A Manual Greek Lexicon of the New Testament.* 3rd Ed. (Edinburgh, Scotland: T. &. T. Clark, 1937).

Douglas A. Foster, Paul M. Blowers, Anthony L. Dunnavant & D. Newell Williams, Eds., *The Encyclopedia of the Stone-Campbell Movement.* (Grand Rapids, MI: William B. Eerdmans Publishing Company, 2004).

Jean L. McKechnie, Gen. Ed., *Webster's New Universal Unabridged Dictionary.* 2nd Ed. (New York: Simon and Schuster, 1979).

Joseph Henry Thayer, *Greek-English Lexicon of the New Testament.* (Grand Rapids, MI: Zondervan Publishing Company, n.d.).

The Catholic Encyclopedia: An International work of Reference on the Constitution, Doctrine, Discipline and History of the Catholic Church. Charles G. Herbermann, Edward A. Pace, et. al., Editors. 16 Vols. (New York: Encyclopedia Press, Inc., 1913).

BOOKS

Abilene Christian College Lectures. Authority in Christianity. (Austin, TX: Firm Foundation Publishing Company, 1960).

Adam Clarke, *Commentary and Critical Notes on the Bible.* 6 Vols. (Nashville, TN: Abingdon Press, n.d.).

Eusebius, *Ecclesiastical History.* Reprint. (Grand Rapids, MI: Baker Book House, 1958).

Everett Ferguson, *The Church of Christ: A Biblical Ecclesiology for Today.* (Grand Rapids, MI: William B. Eerdmans Publishing Company, 1996).

_____. *Church History: From Christ to Pre-Reformation.* Vol. 1. (Grand Rapids, MI: Zondervan, 2005).

Edward T. Hiscox, *The Standard Manual for Baptist Churches.* (Chicago, IL: American Baptist Publication Society, 1951).

Charles M. Jacobs, *The Story of the Church.* (Philadelphia, PA: Muhlenberg Press, 1925).

M. C. Kurfees, *Instrument Music in the Worship*. (Nashville, TN: Gospel Advocate Company, 1950).

Kenneth Scott Latourette, *A History of the Expansion of Christianity*. 7 Vols. (Grand Rapids, MI: Zondervan Publishing House, 1970).

T. M. Lindsay, *The Church and the Ministry in the Early Centuries*. (London: Hodder and Stoughton, 1903).

James M. Mathes, *Works of Elder B. W. Stone*. (Cincinnati, OH: Moore, Wilstach, Keys and Company, 1859).

Frank S. Mead, *Handbook of Denominations in the United States*. 4th Ed. (Nashville, TN: Abingdon Press, 1965).

John Lawrence Mosheim, *Ecclesiastical History*. 2 Vols. Reprint. (Rosemead, CA: Old Paths Book Club, 1959).

Augustus Neander, *General History of the Christian Religion and Church*. 8th Ed. Translated by Joseph Torrey. (Boston, MA: Crocker and Brewster, 1847).

Albert Henry Newman, *A Manual of Church History*. 2 Vols. (Chicago, IL: American Baptist Publication Society, 1957).

Philip Schaff, *History of the Christian Church*. 8 Vols. (Grand Rapids, MI: W. B. Eerdmans Publishing Company, 1953).

J. W. Shepherd, *The Church, The Falling Away, and The Restoration*. (Nashville, TN: Gospel Advocate Company, 1954).

Barton W. Stone, *The Christian Messenger*. 14 Vols. Reprint. (Fort Worth, TX: Star Bible Publications, 1978).

Rex A. Turner, Sr., *Biblical Theology: Fundamental of the Faith*. Rev. Ed. (Montgomery, AL: Amridge University Press, 2010).

Marvin R. Vincent, *Word Studies in the New Testament*. 4 Vols. Reprint. (Grand Rapids, MI: Wm. B. Eerdmans Publishing Co., 1946).

Williston Walker, *A History of the Christian Church*. Revised by Cyril Richardson, Wilhelm Paulk and Robert Handy. (New York: Charles Scribners' Sons, 1959).

Charles Crossfield Ware, *Barton Warren Stone, Pathfinder of Christian Union; a Story of His Life and Times*. (St. Louis, MO: Bethany Press, 1932).

Earl Ervin West, *The Search for the Ancient Order*. 3 Vols. (Nashville, TN: Gospel Advocate Company, 1949).